The

Chocolate

Persian

An Experiment in Archaeo-humor

Jonathan Elias

Illustrations by Alexis Gessner
and Jonathan Elias

The author gratefully acknowledges a special group of persons to whom he is indebted for interactions inspiring some of the humor in this work. These are Eve Gordon Elias, Alexis Gessner, Ruth Gordon, Allison Hedges, Rob Hoppa, Salima Ikram, Randy Lykins, and Tamás Mekis. Donald P. Ryan is the only member of the group whose last name begins with a letter found in the second half of the alphabet, so he deserves special mention.

For mysterious kindnesses transmitted during the era leading up to the book's appearance, the author thanks Deborah Elias-Smith and Mr. Les Smith, Betty Unruh, Dona Shreve, Alex Klales, Lori Lupton and Tess Gerritsen.

Above all others, the author places Carter Lupton, without whom it is unlikely that any morsel of *The Chocolate Persian* would have come together for the reader's enjoyment.

ISBN-13: 978-1482375893
ISBN-10: 1482375893

To my parents—

Art and Norma

Table of Contents

Chapter 1

A Necessary Lubricant

There's Always Time for Humor

The book that you are about to read contains humorous short essays on history and archaeology. At least these are the intended contents. I can tell you that there are other aspects to the book as well, most of these being reflections on time itself.

Inasmuch as book introductions are supposed to be advertisements persuading readers that they have made an intelligent choice of fare for their brains (and in me as its creator), I will move in that direction. To my readership (i.e., the three or four history buffs who I hope are still reading at this point), I declare that I have done my best to ensure that you will be entertained. To that end, I have brought to the fore all my natural facetiousness to make this book truly readable for you.

First off, and I am not being facetious here, I promise to be tolerant of all of your quirks. For example, I accept that some of you out there may own reproduction Greek hoplite helmets and occasionally put them on. I will never ask you why you do so. I accept your choices as your own and admit that in the days before such helmets were widely available (you can now get them for around $79.99), I spent a full day trying to make one out of aluminum foil. It flopped over and provided poor protection from the broomstick lances directed at it.[1] While adjusting the right cheek piece during a mock combat, I sustained serious cuticle damage when an

---

[1] My parents, concerned for my safety during my brief career as an amateur armorer, and always ready to spoil me, purchased a factory-made breastplate and helmet to replace my aluminum foil one, but in those days all they could get was Roman centurion gear with embarrassingly protrusive nipples and a very un-Roman yellow plume. I blushed to wear it out-of-doors, and became averse to creative anachronism; other side effects being that to this day, I dislike things with plumes or objects remotely smacking of *kitsch*.

opponent struck my un-armored hand. That this wound continues to haunt me shall remain a story for another time. Right now, I will continue making advertising declarations.

There is no other book like this one. At the same time, I present the following disclaimer: Any one of the three or four of you out there looking to experience the massive CGI[2] overload quality of other people's history books, look elsewhere. I cannot claim that my writing style, even when I pull out all the stops when drafting my very best word pictures, can create images equivalent to scenes showing twelve Tolkien Orcs simultaneously exploding after being crushed by lucky trebuchet shots lobbed outside the walls of Minas Tirith. Similarly, I must deny unsubstantiated rumors that I am capable of staging convincing special effects of any kind, even rudimentary pyrotechnic ones like making

---

[2] In my opinion, next to IRS and AARP, CGI has got to be the most important semi-modern acronym.

Gumby melt. I have tried this, and it simply produces a green blob on the carpet with black stringy vapor above that sort of just hangs there smelling funky.

On the plus side, these pages do include a few interesting black and white illustrations. The original idea behind these images was to gain a wider audience by working into them subtle hieroglyphic clues which, if properly deciphered, would help one to select the winning number of the *Mega Millions* lottery game. This proved impractical, however, because of time constraints related to getting this book to publication. It was just too difficult to translate the winning numbers into subtle hieroglyphic clues quickly enough, and things bogged down. I kept the illustrations for purely sentimental reasons.

My plan is to make up for the lack of decent CGI by adding in sound effects here and there, and always when the reader least expects it. I hope this works. (Foley artist: insert sounds resembling muffled applause from six or eight hands, one of which is faltering due to old cuticle damage re-aggravated at a hibachi restaurant last Friday).[3]

Understand that I am *compelled* to present these stories. Every one of them poured out of me as responses to a world which is moving way too fast for conventional historical or archaeological writing. In fact, each of the essays attempts to "get at" *unwritten history*—those interesting aspects of events and time periods which are rarely talked about, and tend to be eclipsed by the supposedly Big Things that are so important.

---

[3] I walked into the restaurant with some friends, and gently placed my hand upon the granite countertop of our hibachi table. In a scene out of Greek tragedy, I lightly grazed an ancient fault line in the granite. A fragment detached and I caught it, but not before my cuticle, injured those many years before, had been torn anew from its moorings.

I am happy to add that this is not a book which can be advertised as being about time travel, even though it deals with that subject a lot. Nor can it be called a cookbook despite the fact that many of the stories include vignettes associated with food. (But more on the food thing once I've had my lunch). I have learned through the years not to mention the words "time travel" aloud in my house (understand: in the presence of my wife) unless I want an argument to erupt. The following refrains soon fill the air: "time travel is inherently illogical," "it always ends badly," "it doesn't make any sense," "the guy ends up dead," "it's really depressing," "the butterfly ends up dead," and last but not least, "it's not possible for Old Spock and Young Spock to meet one another!"

In spite of the acrimony, these arguments over time travel, heated though they may be, have been enormously productive and have influenced much of what appears in this book. This is a book for people who, like my wife and me, want to think about things in a different way. It's a book for people who love history and who think they're special because of it. It's a book for people who enjoy the feeling they get when recognizing the existence of meaningful coincidence in their lives, and wonder how this stuff happens.

But believe me, as much as I am interested in time, time travel is not my goal; I am interested in using my unique experiences in the stream of time to make you laugh. I can't help the fact that I witnessed the investiture of Sammy Davis Jr. into the Knights of Malta, any more than I can explain why I was present when the mime Marcel Marceau had his luggage stolen in Chicago and started shouting hysterically. All I know is that these kinds of historical oddities are unnecessarily overridden by a lot of boring crap, and that it is up to me to dredge them back up for your enjoyment and edification.

Bemusement is the straightest route to some kind of historical epiphany that I can think of. Humor can help us endure the pain of our studies. For example, there are those archaeological objects out there that seem to have been produced as inducements for scholarly insanity, a well-known Egyptian example being the Narmer Palette,[4] the true meaning of which remains coded.[5] Its unfathomability is surpassed

---

[4] Narmer, that much-vaunted unifier of historic Egypt, is shown on this object wearing the White Crown, which we now see as resembling a standard bowling pin.

[5] I recently attended a conference where a well-known archaeologist (kind'uv a retired one) decided he had unraveled the mystery of the Narmer Palette and presented his thoughts on the topic. People crushed others on their way in to hear him speak. He said virtually nothing of real novelty, but his fame garnered him a "standing room only" crowd just the same. I pity the young grad student speaking across the hall about something interesting but less mysterious. He had an audience of three.

only by the bloody "Phaistos disk." The latter object from Crete is surely mysterious, being peppered with flowers, little heads wearing feathered hats, and other symbols arranged in a spiral pattern meant to torment us. You won't find me trying to translate it. I think it is probably little more than a version of *Candy Land* for Minoans. What is the Minoan equivalent for "Ice Cream Floats," I wonder? Its very existence is an affront to human intellect, since it is likely to eat up lifetimes should anyone be foolhardy enough to dedicate themselves to the disk's decipherment. However, when one discovers, through the power of the internet, that there's a company out there mass-producing copies of the pesky thing in aluminum (@ $165.00 each), one begins to understand its true significance: pure humor.

I suppose this kind of thing has been going on since the beginning of recorded history. No doubt Narmer himself (Master of the White Crown) moonlighted as a CEO of his own corporation, making cheesy products like cement ashtrays when he wasn't occupied braining the Lower Egyptians.

History and archaeology may not always be about funny things, but on some level, studies of time and time periods can be beneficially approached through humor. At any rate, I think laughter is a necessary lubricant in historical and archaeological research, and ask my readers to appreciate this point of view while digesting my essays. End of advertisement.

Chapter 2
The Doughnut Dialectic
Time Machines and Fun Food

Believe me when I say that I have wasted more time discussing time travel than most people. I have a close and brilliant friend, devoted to the study of Sherlock Holmes (my code name for him is "Mycroft") who has worked at a museum for nearly 40 years. He is an expert on H.G. Wells and tons of other things besides. Just the other day during a trip into Milwaukee, he discussed time travel with me in depth—not that his timing was very good; I was very tired from having had almost no sleep before a 6:15 AM flight, and so was not really fully awake. As we sped along in his sleek SUV from Billy Mitchell Field toward downtown, his initial thoughts developed into a minor Phillipic.

I think that his argument went something like this: In H.G. Wells' *The Time Machine*, at least in the movie version, the time machine is switched on and disappears and then ends up in the future, but it hasn't moved at all. His argument, which I really like, is that if we stand there motionless (never leaving the room with the machine in it), we should see the machine for the rest of our lives. Yet we don't. My conclusion is: as long as the machine disappears, we believe in time travel; we believe that it has gone to another time. If it actually did so, it would probably be generating very high speeds, and the friction created by the mechanism would likely incinerate the room, house, and any idiots standing around waiting to see if the machine actually would disappear (i.e., Mycroft and me). For that matter, anybody in the machine would also get fried. More important still is the question overlooked by physicists throughout the ages: If the machine stays in the same place (part of Wells' story and we're standing there next to it), we have to ask ourselves why we would want to go there? At least this is how I sometimes feel about the neighborhood I live in. Hopefully, time is some other place without an IRS. Then again, even the IRS ceases to be relevant to those getting fried by their time machines.

The conversation had a major effect on my thinking—to wit, for safety reasons, we humans need to focus on inventing a time machine that doesn't work using speed. By the way, during the discussion, Mycroft also attacked the notion that Superman could turn back time simply by spinning the planet Earth in reverse. I think it has something to do with the Sun continuing to do whatever it usually does in spite of Superman's efforts. For some reason, he upset me when he said this, but I had to admit that he was right.

At that very moment, the conversation switched to the subject of what kinds of doughnuts were being featured at the museum coffee shop that day. Was this the same mighty brain that had, just moments before, conquered the mysteries of time? The change of topic was abrupt enough to cause me to doubt whether he could still properly operate the car. To my relief, a reassuring sense of humor infected his speech, so I remained on the passenger's side rather than unlatch the seatbelt, tuck my body like a rolled up pangolin and take a high-speed tumble out the door. Besides, I thought it just possible that, given the powers of Mycroft's mind and his mystical tendencies, there was a connection between doughnuts and time (like pyramids and Freemasonry), so I listened and carefully contemplated the deeper meaning of the museum's doughnut schedule:

Monday: Chocolate Long John w/custard filling

Tuesday: Chocolate Persian[6]

Wednesday: Chocolate Cake Doughnut

Thursday: Chocolate Long John w/buttercream
    filling.

Just as we were getting to Friday, we
swerved to avoid heavy traffic and lost the thread
of the conversation. I think we can probably
assume that Fridays involved some kind of
cruller—an awful-sounding word which entered
the flow of his speech at this point, and although
I might have been mistaken, I was hearing the
quickly muttered word "cruller" in what was
really an under-the-breath expletive directed at
another driver. In any case, the cruller is a type
of doughnut of Dutch extraction perceived by

---

[6] When mentioning chocolate Persians, Mycroft never
neglects to inform me that "Persian" is a corruption of
"Pershing" and that this type of doughnut was named in
honor of the American general of WWI vintage.

Mycroft as being (in his own words) "nonsense." Research has shown that his opinion is shared by the Dunkin Donuts Corporation, which discontinued crullers in 2003 as being too labor-intensive to produce in its machines. Only the French cruller survives to represent the type within the chain's menu.[7] Why it wasn't triaged like its Dutch cousin, I cannot say.

As Mycroft nudged the car slowly forward into traffic, my mind began to race: Didn't Einstein once say that time and space together were a continuum that, if carefully analyzed, would reveal that the universe took the form of a cruller? No, he never did. Nor did he ever consider that a properly constituted universe designed by a beneficent god who never threw dice would have lots of chocolate frosting, intermixed liberally between time and space to

---

[7] http://en.wikipedia.org/wiki/Cruller

make existence in a multiplicity of worlds more flavorful.

While I couldn't exactly agree that crullers were complete nonsense, I personally think that crullers are not of this earth to begin with, and were placed here by time travelers from the future. I had to admit that their inherent complexity would probably result in their extinction, with or without the frosting. We're just not ready to understand them. One thinks upon the humble dodo of Mauritius, the disappearance of which still angers me to this day. Couldn't you macho men have left a few of these birds alive? The pathetic cruller is simply nature's next dodo.

The vital discovery is this: time and invisibility are linked after all! Given enough time, we can be absolutely certain that everything, like dodos and crullers, will disappear; everything, that is, except the time machine.

Chapter 3
Stereotypes and Dalmatians
The Soul and Immortality

One morning, thinking myself very clever, I said to my wife: "I'm a stereotype of myself!" Not losing a second, she replied: "Aren't we all?" Although she (Eve is her name) was clearly joking, her quip set me to wondering whether we human beings are in the final analysis merely copies of someone or something else. More importantly, I was moved by the exchange to begin work on a miniature but special project (MBSP)[8] to ascertain once and for all whether I might be only a copy rather than the original of myself. It was an odd question to be sure, but a worthwhile one which propelled me into some strange areas as I pressed onward to discover the

---

[8] The acronym MBSP refers to any time-destroying activity that starts off small but eventually grows in inverse proportion to its apparent value until it eventually replaces one's original set of tasks.

answer. And no, the answer is not suggested by the question: "Am I not my own father's son?" which I believe originated from a rightfully-ignored section of the Bible.

Years ago, I had the opportunity to study an Egyptian coffin that struck me as very pretty but at the same time very strange, though I wasn't able to put into words why I thought it was strange, so in preparing this essay, I asked for help from my illustrator, a talented woman in her early 20's (Alexis is her name) whom I had hired to assist me in various capacities and now was assigned tasks related to the MBSP. I asked her to describe what she was illustrating. She chuckled at first and then insisted that I, as a professional Egyptologist, could do a better job of describing things than she could ever do. I explained that Egyptologists are by in large too conventional in their vocabulary to really get to the heart of the matter. She shook her head "No."

I asked her again "Pretty please." She politely requested that I stop interrupting her while she was working. Disappointed but not dismayed, I pressed on with my side of the work, though the more I thought about her reproof, something began to gnaw at me. Perhaps she had subconsciously identified me as the copy of myself, and ignored my cries for assistance because mere copies weren't really worth helping.

The image on the middle of the chest of the coffin which my illustrator drew but refused to describe to me (the mere copy of myself) showed a goddess with broad, outstretched wings dappled with plumage. Her arms were bent and she supported in each hand two birds with human heads. The goddess was Nut ("Noot") who represented the sky and was normally on Egyptian coffins below the collar about mid-chest. The birds represented the concept known as a *Ba*, which is usually translated as "soul."

As far as we can make out, the *Ba* was the real personality, the part that anyone would want to have around, if they wanted you around at all. Each person had just one. This personality element was liberated from the body at death and became kind of rudderless for a period of time, if not completely lost. The goal of mummification was to turn the body into a beautiful perfect form which would be so attractive that the soul would find its way back to the body (i.e., the mummy) and eventually re-enter at the level of the heart, which is where the imagery was placed on the coffin lid. Once in, the *Ba* would re-animate the body, and presto—reincarnation would occur. There is nothing at all strange in this scenario, but then I thought: *This coffin has two Bas on it—and this was odd.*

It was getting close to lunch and I had a sneaking suspicion that Alexis might be getting hungry too, so I suggested that we break. After she left, I thought I would check a few sources to see what was going on. I found that the Dalmatian Egyptologist Louis Vico Žabkar (1914–1994) had preceded me in my 2011 research on the *Ba* by about 43 years. I was crest-fallen and ready to abandon the MBSP. Yet once I had succeeded in discovering that Dalmatia simply meant Yugoslavia and that 43 years was still less than half a century, I renewed my search for the truth. I determined that Žabkar's basic view was the same as mine had become—that the *Ba* concept goes beyond that of the "soul" in the conventional Western sense—that a *Ba* was more like our personal essence, the stuff that makes each of us who we are. Žabkar put it more forcefully: "There is no internal dualism in man."[9]

Looking back at the designs on the coffin, I noticed small hieroglyphic texts next to each of the *Ba* drawings. Next to the one on the right, the texts read: "Strong upon earth." The left one had texts by it that I translated "The Ba is with Ra in heaven." (Remembering that Ra is the god of the sun and pretty much all-powerful in ancient Egypt, I felt that the left hand *Ba* had gotten the better deal). Then later on I wondered: So which is it? When a person dies, isn't the *Ba* supposed

---

[9] Louis V. Žabkar, <u>A Study of the Ba Concept in Ancient Egyptian Texts</u>, Studies in Ancient Oriental Civilization 34, Chicago,1968:113.

to find its body and re-animate it or something? If so, what is the *Ba* doing up in heaven with Ra?

At this point, an email arrived from a museum contact of mine who had called me several weeks before, eager to have me reserve some exhibit dates for her so that we could ship our big show south the following spring. At the time, this was a huge boost to morale and made us all very happy. The email read: "Everyone here is really excited, but we have to decline for now because of the current budget. How about next year?" This I thought was a typical *windgy* museum response in the Age of Email—blaming nebulous budget troubles for everything without talking about anything of substance or trying to address issues by talking at all. (Foley artist: insert flushing sound). It's nice to know that everyone was "really excited" though.

Then I had a eureka moment regarding the scenes on the coffin. The *Ba* has to be "strong on earth" because almost nothing on earth goes according to plan (Yes, this is true, no matter how "excited" everyone may have been). Take death, for example. Beyond being a general downer, it usually conflicts with our main set of plans, excepting wills and suicide notes and certain insurance policies. As human beings, we basically want to live and be happy. These are the paramount goals of our species. Only three things on earth are guaranteed to conflict with these objectives: (1) emails from organizations where everyone is said to be "excited" but who are in reality ineffectual, [10] (2) death, and perhaps the worst of all (3) really bad movies unrecognized as such.[11]

---

[10] An important cryptological principle emerges here: Any communication that emphasizes how excited people are is actually a ruse used to conceal a complete <u>lack</u> of enthusiasm; At the risk of sounding pessimistic, if not twisted, we must note another finding: the word "everyone" may refer to a very small contingent indeed.

[11] War could be added to the list, but as its main configurations are so complex and disturbing, I refuse to let

"Really bad movies unrecognized as such" are almost by definition highly touted, but routine analysis actually shows them to be based so heavily on sleight of hand effects or odd bits and pieces of older stories that are so clichéd that they cannot be survived. Often the originals

---

them overwhelm this essay. War can be treated in the same category with death or with really bad movies unrecognized as such.

were not always so original either. A good example of this is *The Red Violin,* a 1998 movie which expects the viewer to sit almost forever while an ingenious forensic scientist tries before an important auction to determine why the violin is red. This is fine so far as it goes, but it strains credulity to accept that the scientist is unable to infer (until just before movie's climactic finish) that some early instrument maker had added blood to the violin varnish.

I guess the point of it all is that violins, unlike the people who own them, are almost eternal. At the same time, they benefit from human frailty and are somehow enriched as they are passed again and again through the hands of the living. This was cinematically proven for Rolls-Royces, too. In a 1965 release (*The Yellow Rolls-Royce*), the multiple lives of an English luxury car are visualized, but here the yellow enamel of the new vehicle was eventually over-painted with some dull color once the car arrived in war-torn Yugoslavia, hiding its original character. The audience is brought to tears at the thought that no one ever had the time or inclination to wax its shapely body. Surely there must have been a decent wax somewhere in the old Yugoslavia, or was this indeed a desolate, carnauba-free Europe? Fortunately, relief is implied at the film's end and we all can leave the theatre hopeful that extensive body work will at last take place and that the vehicle's showroom finish will re-emerge. As I awoke from my "old movie stupor," I wondered: might not the vehicle's transformation be a clue to solving riddles concerning the re-discovery of our own inner nature as human beings?

Had I reached a conclusion to my MBSP? Perhaps I had. The earth-bound *Bas* of each of us are no doubt besieged by a spate of bad movies, the kind usually set in wax-free Yugoslavia or featuring emotionally disturbed violin owners. To this, the Egyptians had an answer: one copy to handle the crap, another to kiss the sun—a lucky version of ourselves waiting to shine forth like the bright yellow lacquer of a brand new Rolls Royce.

Chapter 4

Will the Real Indiana Jones Please Sit Down?

Weak Chins, Strong Chins, and the True Identity of Indiana Jones

This essay was started on July 19, 2011. This date is significant as falling exactly one week after I had the first opportunity as an adult to watch the movie *Spartacus* starring Kirk Douglas. Kirk is by far my favorite actor with a severely cleft chin. Beyond this, I have to say that he is far more convincing in the role of the gladiator Spartacus than his co-star Laurence Olivier (a fine chin-clefted actor in his own right) was in the role of the dictator Crassus. Olivier captures the right levels of insane sexual frustration one imagines Crassus to have felt, but he seems to play Crassus incorrectly—intelligent and cerebral; dictators are crafty manipulators, but never really intelligent. In fact, the defining characteristic of dictators is an ability to co-opt and *defeat* intellect. I think also that there is tendency for dictators to have prominent chins, although the cleft element is not essential and the Jaw itself may be Made of Glass.

I had just seen stories published in what were at that moment believable newspapers, relating to the firing of Dr. Zahi Hawass effective July 18th, 2011. As of that instant, Dr. Hawass became the first former Secretary General of the Supreme Council of Antiquities of Egypt, or alternatively (in the language of Mubarak's final government), the first former Minister of State for Antiquities Affairs. (So rapidly did events begin moving that his successor was, within days and for a short time, accurately describable as the second former Minister of State for Antiquities Affairs). At that point, Hawass became the first re-hired first former so-and-so. He was then re-ousted. As incredible as all this sounds, what's more amazing is that in all of this shuffling, the prominence of Hawass' chin went unmentioned.

Dr. Hawass' current status is sad news for some, pleasing news to others, and clearly means something but what that is, no one can say. The list of those in a state of uncertainty probably includes the financial department at National Geographic, which was widely believed to be paying many bills in exchange for access to Egypt's archaeological sites for the production of videos. The meaning of his rise and the lessons learned from his supposed fall will vary according to who is interpreting, like fragments of the distant Egyptian past which experts argue over and which, it may be contended, Hawass thought he was protecting.

One thing is for certain, however: I am incensed over a caption that appeared in one of the papers containing this story which contends that George Lucas consulted Dr. Hawass before creating the character of Indiana Jones.[12] (To quote a favorite expression of a brilliant Hungarian colleague of mine: "I think that this must be seen as bad archaeology." *Úgy gondolom hogy ezt úgy kell tekinteni mint rossz régészet.* I admit that my attempt at translating this expression must be seen as bad Hungarian).

It is common knowledge that Indiana Jones first appeared in film in 1981. Dr. Hawass was born in 1947 and would have been 34 years old at the time of the release of *Raiders of the Lost Ark.* This was also at least 6 years before he received his Ph.D. from the University of Pennsylvania. So how do we see Hawass being consulted by Lucas in the creation of Indy? I would understand very well if Lucas (who I

---

[12] Richard Spencer 'Real Indiana Jones' sacked as keeper of Egypt's heritage' The Telegraph 19 July 2011. http://www.telegraph.co.uk/news/worldnews/africaandindia nocean/egypt/8645356/Real-Indiana-Jones-sacked-as-keeper-of-Egypts-heritage.html. The caption reads: "George Lucas consulted Zahi Hawass before creating the character of Indiana Jones."

believe in 2009 gave Hawass an Indy-style bullwhip) had spoken to him at some point and said: "Hey Zahi, do you want me to publicly compare you to the Indiana Jones character who I created twenty years ago? If I had known you back then, you would surely have inspired me!" If something like this had been said, I could see that such words would begin to slosh around pretty quickly and eventually result in a crazy caption.

We can perhaps understand the confusion shown by the author of the caption. In a perusal of the frequently maligned and more frequently consulted Wikipedia and other articles dealing with Indy's connection to actual archaeologists, one learns practically nothing about who actually inspired the film character. In the standard lists of possible Indy prototypes, the name of the most plausible candidate never appears.

I stumbled upon what seems to be the answer about three years ago when I was asked to prepare a lecture about the ancient civilizations of Mexico. Since my personal library on the topic was a little sparse, I worked hard to buttress my supply of information by checking through old magazines, journal articles, and by surfing the net. The farthest thing from my mind at this time was Indiana Jones. He was the archaeological hero that captivated my imagination in grad school. I had liked the first movie, hated the second movie, and liked the third movie, but had outgrown the whole topic by the time that the fourth movie came out (2008). All the along-the-way stuff, the TV series and the spin-off novellas held no interest for me. I was already well aware, as every film buff had been, of the Indy character's resemblance to Charlton Heston in the role of the occasionally smarmy but otherwise Indy-like Harry Steele in the 1954 feature *Secret of the Incas,* replete with hat, aviator jacket, khakis and so on.

I was surfing around one morning on this Mesoamerica thing and while researching the Olmec civilization, I came across a website containing what looked like B & W images of Indiana Jones. I could see immediately that aspects of Olmec culture had been worked into *Raiders of the Lost Ark*—the little gold figure on the pedestal that he steals and that big rock that rolls after him was about the same dimensions as those huge head sculptures for which the Olmec were justly famous. Obviously, the website creator was playing off the connection and must have thought visitors would like to see some stills from the first (Olmec-y) Indiana Jones movie. Looking again, however, I could tell that the photos were wrong somehow. There was nothing in them that directly mirrored the actual scenes of the movie. When I enlarged the images,

I saw that they were archival photos of a real explorer of the Olmec culture, Matthew Stirling (1896 -1975). But Stirling was pretty damned famous. How could this have gone unnoticed? I can't be the first to make this connection and I bow to anyone before me who has.

Stirling's life and activities mirror Indiana Jones in many ways:

> He is contemporary with Indiana Jones (his birth year 1896 versus 1899 for Jones).

> He wears clothing similar to Indiana Jones. This includes the hat, rugged field shirt, pants and boots.

> He authored a study of giant stone spheres.[13]

---

[13] Stirling, M.W., 1969, An Occurrence of Great Stone Spheres in Jalisco State, Mexico. National Geographic Research Reports. v. 7, pp. 283–286.

He is found in photographs with a big bag like a mail pouch slung by a strap diagonally across his chest. I remember this from the third movie when Indy gets tangled in a tree limb in the shadow of an oncoming tank.

He rides horses.

Running down the hill at the end of the introductory sequence of *Raiders*, which incidentally takes place in Peru (arguably the Amazonian section of Peru) in 1936, Indiana Jones is pursued by blowgun-using "Hovitos." **Stirling studied the head-hunting, blowgun-using Jivaro peoples of Amazonian Equador in the early 1930's, publishing his work in 1938.**

The first movie includes a sea plane. This plane's pilot rescues Indy, who swings from a vine to reach the craft as it waits parked in the river. **Stirling was a pioneer in air reconnaissance. His expedition to New Guinea in 1926 was the first to use an airplane for exploratory survey** work;[14] he had the plane retrofitted with pontoons.[15]

And last but not least, Stirling's wife was named Marion!

This is all very exciting, but what I hope will be an original contribution to science is my observation that George Lucas seems to have incorporated crucial aspects of Matthew Stirling's life and appearance into the character of Indiana Jones *unconsciously*. Is it possible that Lucas had read about Stirling or had seen one of his ethnographic films during childhood or after? Lucas grew up in Modesto, California while

---

[14] See Paul Michael Taylor 2006 "Western New Guinea: The Geographical and Ethnographic Context of the 1926 Dutch and American Expedition." Essay 3: in *By Aeroplane to Pygmyland: Revisiting the 1926 Dutch and American Expedition to New Guinea* Taylor (Washington D.C.: Smithsonian Institution Libraries, Digital Editions, 2006):6, http://www.sil.si.edu/expeditions/1926/essays
[15] Ibid. See also Tony Reichart "Contact: Tales from the era when the Air Age met the Stone Age." 1 Nov. 2004, http:www.airspacemag.com/history-of-flight/contact-nov04.html; http://aerofiles.com/_yz.html

Stirling was a native of Salinas, 116 miles to the south.

HOLD ON A MINUTE!!!

Does any of this kind of analysis really matter? If Modesto were only 58 miles from Salinas, would my theory be any more plausible? Of course it wouldn't. It would just *seem* more plausible, that is to say, more marketable. The issue here is not about what inspired Lucas. It's about what half the world *thinks* it can prove to the *other* half of the world about what *may* have inspired Lucas and gain from the mere conjecture. I'm doing it, too! It's not like it's any big secret anyway. How could it be?

Again the film *Spartacus* comes to mind, you know, that famous next-to-the-next-to-the-last scene where everybody says "I'm Spartacus; No, I'm Spartacus" to protect the identity of the real Spartacus. Any rational being can see that protecting his identity would have been impossible. Are we to believe for one moment that no one had noticed that cleft? Any Roman poet worth his salt would have written odes to that cleft! Furthermore, it was completely within the character of the despotic and sexually frustrated Crassus to have lined up everybody claiming to be Spartacus and had his centurion perform a detailed cleft inspection on each of them. The centurion, being a nicer, less frustrated soul than Crassus, would say (in Latin) "Will the real cleft please stand up?" Or better still, "Will those lacking clefts one inch wide please sit down?" Spartacus would have been left all alone.

In a similar fashion, if we lined up all the potential Indy-inspiring candidates, we would immediately understand Matthew Stirling's absence from the group. Despite a career spanning fifty years and crowned with

achievements worthy of an Indy, his chin —
smooth, un-cleft, and un-chiseled — just never
made the grade.

Chapter 5
Grandpa Bob's Pencil Jar
Film Noir Yarn about an Archaeologist's Love of Stone

Every school child is taught that the Egyptians, while not a Stone Age people, excelled at cutting stone, working in stone, building in stone, etching on stone and grinding flour on stone. They also were good at the moving of stone. As a result of their abilities in the area of moving large pieces of stone, they developed a strange addiction to the creation of some very big statues. Alexis calls these things "Ginormous Stone Carvings."

With all the temples, colossi and obelisks lying around, it is easy to become inured to the small but often very beautiful objects which the Egyptians created from the earliest flowering of their culture: bowls and jars of translucent alabaster, slate, and various types of veined stone which in short hand can be called marble, although Egyptologists hardly ever use that term. Egyptologists for unknown reasons prefer to call their pieces of stone by esoteric petrological terms which no one other than career geologists fully understand. Examples include schist, diabase, greywacke, diorite, and more schist. Egyptologists prefer to say "steatite" where normal people would just say "soapstone."

If one goes to Egypt today, it is difficult to leave the country without acquiring a souvenir object made of "alabaster." In its ancient sources (clustered near a site called Hatnub), this stone is wonderfully veined and produces absolutely gorgeous objects. In its modern sources (clustered near sites unknown), the supposed alabaster produces objects that cause us to wonder if plastic fake butter containers are available for purchase, preferably devoid of their original contents, even if those contents were enriched with Omega-3's.

Beauty is so often lacking from the world. I say this again and again as I move through towns where old wooden fences are torn down for the need of some paint, only to be replaced by PVC modular fencing which sags in the hot sun. It is made to be unpaintable on the theory that bright white is preferable to all other colors. At least we can look ahead to the visual relief afforded by the inevitable development of prosperous algae colonies between the slats.

The beauty dearth is something I have been sensitive to all my life. At the same time, I must confess that despite my addiction to fake butter with Omega-3's and tolerance for its containers when faced by the specter of bad alabaster, I dislike most plastics. Give me something made of good hard stone any day.

For a long time, I thought that I was born with a genetic predisposition toward stone. When I was three or four, I was drawn magnetically to a crumbling stone wall to the left side of my family's driveway on Lindabury Lane and began trying to reconstruct it. It was only after I lifted the first stone back into its position that I realized there was something called gravity and that it made the stone very, very heavy. It smashed my left hand and blood flowed, but my love of stone continued and deepened.[16]

In the days after the hand-smashing event, I traveled a short distance to the home of my grandparents for a weekend stay. It was a big old place with a winding stairway (to me seemingly endless) that led to the second floor where all the bedrooms were. My grandfather operated a store at the time, and this being an era before the advent of home offices, he did his "books" at a desk positioned in the corner of his bedroom. There were always coins around (he had a thing

---

[16] One will recall the infamous "hibachi restaurant incident" referred to in Chapter 1, footnote 3. I would just like to add that the staff there was very nice, and gave me a free Band-Aid and deducted 10% off the check.

for silver dollars), bags for making deposits, bill clips, wrappers and stuff like that. Among the paraphernalia of petty business scattered across this desk was a small rose-colored jar made of veined stone that fascinated me. It held pencils. It was the first true pencil jar I had ever seen— grooved on the outside by an expert in the craft of cutting stone. On many occasions, I emptied it of all contents and held it next to my cheek—it was always colder than the air. Another game was to stick it over my ear to listen into it like one does with a sea shell. I loved that damn thing.

I eventually forgot about it, and went to college, then university and so on. After years of study, I became an Egyptologist, which is usually about studying ancient documents. My experience was entirely different, however, and for me, studying ancient Egypt meant studying stone fragments. I was drawn to the types of

stone they had there—luscious, colorful granites,
basalts and porphyry. What a neat stone-working
civilization! I became a closet rock junkie,
spending my leisure hours studying geology
textbooks.

After years of this, I finally made it to
Egypt as a junior member of an American dig at
one of Egypt's oldest sites, Hierakonpolis, the
hometown of Egypt's first historical ruler, Menes,
a.k.a. Narmer, "Master of the White Crown." It
was not a very well-funded project, and apart
from learning to eat mackerel straight from the
can, I remember a particularly sordid episode
working around a temple entryway. Before
succumbing to dysentery (the common fate of all
who moved off the mackerel and chanced to eat
the friendly villagers' hand-crafted yogurt), I got
to excavate around a huge sculpted chunk of
pink granite that formed the threshold of the
temple's main doorway. The soil around this

block was littered with sandstone fragments from some long-lost slab of wall. Below the layer containing these fragments, there was a stratum of dark soil containing shards of really early pottery from the Predynastic period before 3,000 BC. I had high hopes of discovering stone vessels of the type characteristic of this period, vessels of the finest alabaster veined and striated in glorious patterns of natural beauty (probably from Hatnub). Just as things started to get interesting, however, the dig director, desiring to find objects linked more directly to ancient royalty, reassigned me, and so my appointment with the glories of Predynastic stone vesseldom was missed.[17]

---

[17] This brings me to the subject of what I term "selective archaeology," that is to say, choosing one's favorite period in history and researching that period to the near exclusion of all else. In archaeological parlance, this means hunting down the layers that have the most meaning to us, even if it means annihilating all intervening periods. This may sound a bit prejudicial, but kegs of black powder and

Life goes on for some of us, and everyone else mentioned in this story having died in the meantime (except Eve and Alexis), I came into possession of some objects from my mother's estate. Among the boxes of office supplies taken from her apartment was a small jar. I looked at it as I lifted it from the swirl of ball-point pens and Post-it pads. It was my grandpa Bob's pencil jar! Happiness ensued as I touched it to my cheek and put it over my ear to hear the sea within. I eventually stuck it on the little bookshelf attached to my prefab desk. Looking at it again, I paused (the Egyptologist within me had been activated); it was oddly reminiscent of the kind of jars the Egyptians made during the late Predynastic period, around the time that Menes, a.k.a. Narmer, Master of the White Crown, was roaming around.

---

bulldozers are not entirely unknown in the history of archaeological investigation.

For about a week, I pondered the jar's true nature. Could it be a real antiquity? Or was it just a happy accident, the one case out of a million that a pencil jar was actually made out of some really nice stone? A day after this question came into my mind I received an email from Mycroft, who from time to time sent me news updates relating to Egypt. This morning's news had something to do with a big federal bust of a ring of smugglers who had brought an Egyptian coffin into the US labeled as "antique wood panels."

It wore on me all day and deep into the night. Had my grandfather been a smuggler of rare Predynastic stone vessels labeled as "pencil jars"? I knew that seventy years before this, his business had brought him into contact with a character named Longie Zwillman, a personality during the waning years of Prohibition. My analytical tendencies flared up: Had the

Predynastic stone vessels been shipped
surreptitiously through small inlets off the New
Jersey Coast filled with illicit spirits? Had my
own beloved grandfather masterminded the
"pencil jars caper" in order to get a piece of the
action at the local speak-easy? Then it dawned on
me: I was perhaps nothing more than the
misbegotten scion of a gang of rum-running
thugs. Too exhausted to hypothesize further, I
joined Eve, who had developed the habit of going
to sleep like clockwork, knowing that I would
generally remain awake for about an extra hour
trying to disturb my quietude with inane
theorizing just before bedtime. This time, I had
worked myself into a condition and just fell
asleep.

I dreamt there was a knock on the door
and that two customs officials entered to have a
look around our house. I knew of course that I
was completely innocent, but the dream became

exceedingly sinister in its tones and dimensions, as if F.W. Murnau had been put in charge of the art department.[18] The main focus was the small bookshelf sitting atop my desk.

"So you think you're innocent, eh? Then what's this thing sitting on your desk?" The official directed my attention to the small stone jar with its grooved exterior. The dream reflected accurately that it currently held a paint brush, the cheap kind which leaves bristles in the painted surface every few seconds during the emulsion process. I stuttered back, hesitantly: "You mean my grandpa Bob's pencil jar?" I explained confidently that I had just received it from my mother's estate and that her father had used it as a pencil jar during the Great Depression.

---

[18] The director of the 1922 German Expressionist film *Nosferatu*, the first adaptation of Bram Stoker's *Dracula*.

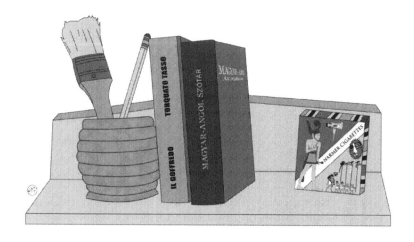

He smelled the jar and detected the pungent aroma of seventy-year-old rum mixed with notes of cherry pencil shavings and graphite. "You're goin' downtown—we ain't stupid, ya know." I quickly tried to demonstrate that it operated like a true pencil jar by depositing a nearby red pencil into its maw. This simply inflamed the situation. I was quickly handcuffed and taken to the station house, or whatever it was.

I felt the heat of a lamp and I kept my eyes closed so as not to be blinded. "Okay you" (he actually called me "you"), we're gonna get to the bottom of this, one way or another." I began to sweat, and then I heard the good cop say to the bad cop: "I think it may be time to blow some smoke in his face. You got any cigarettes? You know, the nasty kind with no filters?"

No filters? This was too much! Remembering my childhood asthma, I quickly struggled to awaken myself from the dream. It was proving difficult to do so as I heard one of the agents say "You don't get away that easy." As I questioned whether it was possible for a dream character to keep me within a dream that I already knew to be a dream, I heard the other agent say "Hey, this thing says Narmer on it!!" I really panicked at this point. How could I have ended up with Narmer's own pencil jar? But then an unexpected sense of relief flowed in upon me—it was laced with delicious hints of melatonin. My pencil jar held no one's interest. The agent had actually been referring to one of the filter-less cigarettes.

Chapter 6

That Time Machine Thing

Philosophical Implications of eBay Buying and Selling

This essay is extremely complex, so if you're feeling even slightly queasy or dehydrated from last night, or think you might have to go to the bathroom soon, you may want to save reading this one for another time. It concerns the time machine <u>thing</u> again (I really want to use the word "idea" here, but I must keep my language simple from now on, since I was recently chastened when I tried using an apparently complicated word like "structure" in conversation with a physician about a blood clot, who decided I was not at the level to employ such vocabulary, and replaced what I thought was a nifty and descriptive word with a more exacting one of his own to describe what appeared in the sample: "the blood clot thing").

Before we return to the essay, please learn from my experience and follow *Safety procedure 137-A for Non-Doctors*—keep your language to less than two syllables when speaking to a physician and use the word "thing" as often as possible, even if you know the real scientific name for what you're talking about; example: "Doc–Might this thing be a blood clot? It's red and looks like an ugly <u>round</u> thing?" *Safety procedure 137-B*, by the way, is even more critical to remember: "Only use the word 'idea' or 'structure' in the company of a physician at the risk of having your co-pay increased."

In past essays, I may have implied that time machines were impossible to manufacture. However, as a result of my research into a variety of topics, I now think that we are quite close to breaking the long-elusive time barrier; I actually think that we have broken the barrier—and I am not talking about that time machine purportedly

invented in the year A.D. 2239 by Dr. J. S. Strauss
which sold on eBay back in 2005.[19] I am talking
about eBay itself. In my opinion, eBay comes
exceedingly close to functioning in the way a
time machine probably should in the area of data
collection and sorting. I think that it is already
widely understood by collectors that eBay can be
used to discover what most rational minds have
discarded or forgotten years ago. eBay to a great
extent is an accumulation point for cast-off
objects. The site works according to what I would
describe as a *serendipity algorithm* which allows
us to trawl through cast-offs which are deposited
through the mysterious workings of a multitude
of minds. It is precisely because a multitude of
minds are involved (and not a dictatorial, over-
arching mind) that the cast-offs (in eBay parlance,

---

[19]Don Tillman's Blog 16 March 2005,
http://www.till.com/blog/archives/2005/03/theres_a_time_m.
html

"items") become re-charged with relevance to the potential time traveler.

What makes eBay items interesting is that they have no use to the sellers, except in terms of becoming fungible; eBay preserves the past because it makes these things less onerous to keep, in that it gives sellers hope that their nearly useless ephemera might be seen as relevant to someone else. (Note: singular overarching minds don't like you using the word "structure," either, but they don't mind imposing one on you).

That someone else is the time traveler.

I dare say that one could keep a blood clot from one's most recent accident in a small beaker, and sell it on eBay for a return. I think furthermore that if one had a beaker they wished to sell, they could manufacture a blood clot (sorry, "blood clot thing") to go inside it to speed up the sale. I am not trying to say that this is unethical—I really want to indicate a process. If one types the words "blood clot" into eBay, one soon discovers that there exists something known as a *Serum Clot Activator tube for blood collection,* and that these are coated with a substance which aids coagulation and helps to separate the blood components, oops, I mean "things."

I maintain that in most internet searches outside of eBay, the unenlightened non-expert would have to do twice as much searching to reach a "relevance point" or eureka moment in their hunt for interesting information. A normal internet search requires that you pre-design your search criteria and by so doing, you limit your search to the neighboring realms of the predictable and atrociously dull. It's like taking an endless walk in an over-55 gated community while eating a packaged granola bar, when one really wants to have pancakes with real maple syrup in a "greasy spoon" filled with affable townsfolk. In other words, many internet searches should actually begin with eBay; it's a source of a more organic, purer form of information which has not yet been trimmed down by an over-arching designer with bland categories for things. eBay allows apparently nonsensical intrusions to go unimpeded, and this process lumps objects together in startling ways. If someone describes something "badly," it ends up with other things which the power freak would want to screen off in order to keep pure—the lack of purity enhances absurdity, which is often fun and enriching.

A search using the words "time machine" on eBay brings one to a DVD entitled: "Bikini Time Machine".[20] It is apparently a film distributed in 2011, released on the historically-important Ides of March. The cover alone is

---

[20] Search dated 17 Aug, 2012 at 10:50 AM.

worth visiting. It is the widescreen version, and this may have been a necessity in view of the subject matter. At this point, if we want to discover more, the internet itself can be consulted directly to learn what we probably already may have assumed—that the film was unrated and its budget did not exceed $500,000.00.[21] I am not entirely sure that the film should be posted on the site, but it reveals something pivotal. The fact that something which has been begging to be forgotten for years can still be unearthed on eBay, should get us researching the *serendipity algorithm* full-time in order to get this time travel "thing" done.

---

[21] http://www.imdb.com/title/tt1777604/business, retrieved 17 August 2012.

Chapter 7

Despotic Humor

Would the Ancient Egyptians have made Good Friends?

I believe on principle that there is absolutely nothing funny about computers. At the same time, they are surely interesting insofar as they have a tendency to do things arbitrarily and on their own which elevates them to the level of those friends we had in our youth—you know, the kind who said they were going to go out to the movies with you, but then ended up going skiing on some mountain with someone else.

This morning, my computer went skiing with someone else.

When I booted up and went online, or thought I did, a pop-up box (I call these things "indoctrination boxes") opened and asked me if I wanted to continue to work offline (this was the computer equivalent of that friend who wanted to go skiing without me). All my modem lights were illuminated in a normal way. I pressed a button that said "connect" (read: "go to the movies with friend"). The computer responded with another box giving me the choice to stay offline (read: "have your friend go skiing without you") or "try again" (read: "wait around pathetically while your friend, unbeknownst to you, has already completed two runs on the expert slope at Sugarbush").

Enough said. I decided to stay offline and write this essay instead.

Now, the Egyptians had no mountains with snow, so they were unable to develop skiing and so leave their movie-loving friends in the lurch. Herein lies an important question: Given that skiing did not exist in their world, would the Egyptians have made good friends?

We all know that the Egyptians get a bad rap; history seems to have written somewhere that this great ancient culture had nothing resembling a sense of humor. In the movies relating to the ancient Egyptians (and this is true of the Hollywood portrayal of adherents to most ancient cultures), people never laugh in a modern sense ("hey, that was funny—snicker snicker") but only in a despotic sense.

What do I mean by "laugh in a despotic sense"? First of all, it's generally the kind of laughter spewed out during acts of vengeance, or the kind of humor produced by the feeling that having the upper hand gives you special rights. Think of that ugly Eli Wallach, laughing at good Clint Eastwood in the spaghetti western *The Good, the Bad and the Ugly*. Clint and Eli are supposed to be something like friends in this movie, but in a famous scene, poor Clint is dying of thirst while Eli Wallach basically spends his time laughing and drinking from a canteen, sadistically wasting the water while salty sand covers Clint's crusty eyes. Clint gets majorly sunburned in that movie! It just isn't that funny and not all that friendly, either. I can almost hear Wallach say to Clint: "Do you want to connect or continue to work offline?" uttering a despotic bellylaugh while spilling out more precious water into the desert sand. (Foley artist: insert soundtrack from *The Good, the Bad and the Ugly*: Doo-da-doo-da-doo, Wah Wah Wah).

The American Old West is very big on this type of humor, but it isn't good for one's soul and no one would really want to have Wallach's character as a friend. The fact that the Old West was generally unfriendly and despotic comes from what may one day become an established fact: most settlers to Old Western places were already suffering severe PTSD from participation in the American Civil War, or were raised by such people.

In Old West movies and in movies about the ancient world as well, despotic humor generally involves alcoholic beverages. Hollywood long ago discovered while developing ancient villains that it's much easier to laugh despotically and with gusto after imbibing wine (preferably a Phoenician merlot and preferably from an over-sized goblet). It gets even easier when the drinking is done straight from the amphora. However, I have noted again and again that vintage Hollywood felt it absolutely necessary to get moralistic about the swigging of wine, and its directors therefore create scenes in which villains (mostly of the petty variety) are made to pay for their intemperance and displays of despotic humor. In these scenes, the villains don't become pleasantly tipsy; they almost invariably become blind drunk, fall asleep and suffer some form of humiliation. The form of the humiliation meted out to the now drooling and unconscious lesser villains ranges from getting their faces licked clean by dogs, to being awakened and publicly embarrassed by the smiling Spartacus who surrounded the camp which the lesser villains left improperly defended due to overindulgence in Phoenician merlot. Shame!

Leaving the Egyptians to one side for the moment, I wish to declare that in marked contrast to the petty villains described above, the Supervillains of the ancient world were able to hold their wine relatively well. This is particularly true of Xerxes I of Persia who seems never to be the worse for wine while marching through and destroying what he can of Greece in 480 BC, even though some sources reveal him to have thrown a big drunken bash back home in

Persia before setting out. His sobriety is not surprising, for ancient Supervillains in the movies (like Xerxes) have absolutely no friends at all and therefore need to be awake enough to identify potential assassins. It is also a benefit to the moviegoer that they remain awake to appreciate the activities of the dancing girls and scantily-clad gymnastic camp followers which fill up needed minutes in the otherwise wispy screenplay. These minutes are, by the way, punctuated intermittently by breathy conversations peppered with deep plans and outbursts of despotic humor by speakers consuming prodigious amounts of wine.

There is a special language here that carries over into all kinds of film genres. In the case of pirate movies, the writers substitute cheap rum for the wine. In classic Old West movies, rot-gut is consumed, the word "varmint" is frequently used, and one's foes are called by a

color known in 19th century America as *yella*. In
the series *Deadwood,* words are used that cannot
be repeated, and these words are applied to
friends as well as foes.

It has become clear to me that a lot of
these ancient world villains were created at a
time when alcohol flowed through the streets of
Hollywood, and despots comparable to Xerxes (or
that bad saloon guy in *Deadwood*) actually ran
the studios. I also think it very possible that the
various kinds of movies highlighting despotic
humor depict, in time-altered form, real
relationships that existed between the directors,
screenwriters and others that actually made the
films. Screen writers tortured by the movie
moguls and hounded by the directors would
have had a field day casting their enemies in the
role of an evil Persian king, or wicked pharaoh,
although I have noted that pharaohs, even the
wicked ones, rarely drink wine in the movies.

A strong case in point: Yul Brenner playing the 19th dynasty pharaoh Ramesses II in what is arguably the role he was born to play, is never shown drinking wine. I think that this is significant because we're supposed to think he's at least moderately evil, but he just isn't. How do we stay mad at Ramesses? He doesn't really torture poor Moses. And although Moses is exiled to the wilderness of Sinai, Ramesses doesn't *pull an Eli Wallach* on him or anything, and Moses never really gets even a mild suntan during his desert sojourn or even the faintest hint of a crusty eye. Ramesses could have killed Moses, but he lets him connect without even re-booting.

Although I always root for Moses & Co., there is no way I can see Ramesses as bad. He ain't no Xerxes. While it may be true that he refuses to change the evil aspects of the kingdom that he's inherited, it certainly doesn't mean that he is really a bad person—he's just not a forward-looking kind of guy. He's set in his ways, that's all. I even think that he might have made a pretty good friend in spite of his egotistical qualities and cagey behaviors. His humor is not very despotic; it's better characterized as *facetious,* or clever. He doesn't even have to speak sometimes to be clever. There is a great scene in *The Ten Commandments* where Moses is being questioned by a suspicious Sety I, who wonders why the temple granaries have been raided without his permission. As each perilous question posed by Sety mounts up in the indictment against Moses, Ramesses drops a weight onto a scale that's in the room. Each clank of the scale is a period in another damning sentence.

Now, this is clever and it can even be said to be charming. I would love to have a friend like that. Moses should have, too. He really missed an opportunity here for a truly great relationship.

Just think of all the laughs. This is what friendship is all about—laughs. I have a friend who I love being facetious with. To test whether she can see that I am not completely serious about anything, she often ends up saying "You're full of s---, Jonathan." It makes me laugh, most of all because I like the way she says the name "Jonathan" (in her classy British accent).

Moses is never facetious and never tells Ramesses that "he's full of s---." Silent, sullen types like Moses are real trouble—they're never funny, not even in a despotic way, and they don't know how to make or keep friends. He doesn't understand what a friend is, or how to forgive. He's not even into the dancing girls, either, and he leaves his host to climb some mountain or other. The Burning Bush is cool and all, but hey, has anybody seen that Xerxes lately? This party needs help.

How did this happen to poor Moses? He could've been a real fun guy. He was just too judgmental, I guess. For years I thought that skiing was the root of all evil —a real friend-buster. The problem is not with the skiing —it's with all that other stuff up on the mountain.

Chapter 8
The Case of the Man-Eating Scarab
Egyptian Magic and Computer Gaming

I don't know much about gaming, but one day I came across some articles on the subject while searching for information on scarabs, those dung beetle-shaped amulets so popular in ancient Egypt which must exist in the millions world-wide. My mission was to decipher a particularly cryptic text inscribed on the back of one of these for a close friend who had sent me a couple of images via the internet. I found no information of any relevance to this quest, but because of all the searches, I was now aware that a powerful warlock in the gaming world can choose to wear a scarab pendant which can be used "to conjure up storms of peaceful scarabs." I was excited by the prospect of seeing such a storm, but I was quite frankly perplexed by the issue since I couldn't quite make out why anyone (most of all a gamer) would want to deposit a bunch of peaceful scarabs on anyone. Many of the gamers in the discussion group I chanced upon wondered the same thing. I also must note that while I researched how storms of peaceful scarabs benefitted fantasy gamers, my computer was attacked by a severe, opportunistic virus classed as an Exploit Kit Variant Activity dispatched by somebody named "Morry."

I'm not sure yet who this "Morry" is, but on a lark, I decided to investigate the sinister cross-linkages connected with the word "scarab" to see if the blessed beetle had led me into this snare. I used scientifically precise investigative methods. Typing the words "Morry" and "scarab" into a search engine, I came upon a Twilight Zone episode in which a scarab beetle is used by a mysterious and beautiful woman named Pamela Morris (a Cleopatra look-alike with 1960's style penciled-in eyebrows) to suck the youth out of unsuspecting male visitors to her apartment. She uses this stolen life energy to achieve immortality. And why should she not? Even though she's really weird and spacey, she should get to survive, too, especially if she has a really good strategy to do so. Secondarily, it seems only right that the rest of her keep pace with those indestructible eyebrows. In similar fashion, it seems doubly right that the virus "Morry" should be allowed to suck the life substance out of my hapless laptop.

Insects are not my passion, but I am proud to announce that lately it has been my policy to avoid them rather than to smash them on sight. In a recent discussion with my wife, we decided that this was an intelligent policy and certainly good for one's karma, but that exceptions should be made for any spiders with visible fangs, especially the one that my mother-in-law suspects is living in the overhead lamp in her bedroom and which she blames for an odd outbreak of bites all over her arm. Whatever did the biting did so during the night.

At the risk of sounding like the Transylvanian inn-keeper (*hazigazda*) probably named Bela who speaks to the prim Englishman (either Renfield or Harker) at the beginning of the original *Dracula,* I can tell you that many years before and in that very same bedroom, my wife was attacked and her upper arm was viciously mauled by an unseen enemy. I now declare that she was bitten during a full moon: *bei sze vulf insekt, zat alle man feeren.* His name cannot be pronounced by living people even using the best available Germano-Transylvanian *patois.* All we know is this: the bites were left in the shape of an anchor. We call this incident "the Anchor Attack" and to this very day, we call this 1-inch-high mark "the Anchor."

For a long time, I have accepted, rightfully so, the notion that my wife is the real anchor person of our household. I'm a quasi-creative type and therefore way too volatile most of the time to be of much use. In a certain way, the vicious monster who attacked her that night was simply giving her its own stamp of approval of her positive "anchoring" status—its version of the old USDA choice stamp once seen on red meat or the barbed wire tattoos seen on the upper arms of people who are viewed as good biking companions.

The anchor mark is a sign of distinction in this case. I occasionally still ask my wife (more than twenty years after the attack occurred) "How's the anchor doing?" She usually replies that it's doing fine, to which I say "that's good." For the reader's edification, this is a type of conversation which we classify as "banter." It helps diffuse stress when, for whatever reason, we are feeling ill-at-ease. When our electrical impulses are screwed up, we simply resort to some kind of banter and everything magically becomes better. We particularly like paint color banter. It goes something like this: Person 1 says: "Wouldn't a nice warm tan be better in this room than that harsh yellow?" to which Person 2 replies: "Definitely, and isn't it interesting how light in this room looks different than it does in the den?"

Someone determined long ago that the world's favorite banter is "weather banter." Without it, I'm quite certain that we'd all be at each other's throats within thirty seconds. Far and away my favorite type of banter is "everything magically becomes better banter," which is banter about the healing effects of the bantering process itself. This kind of banter is very effective because it declares to the universe that, regardless of our impending depression, for the time being we'll simply plaster over the psychological equivalent of the Grand Canyon with emotional duct tape and huge amounts of joint compound and then begin sanding before the incredibly lumpy mass has dried.

It may be "scarab banter" to say this, but it has always been a balm to my soul to know that scarabs were in no way involved in the Anchor Attack on my wife. This may conflict, however, with what is now a common misconception about the scarabs enjoyed by the ancient Egyptians—that they are man-eaters.

I already knew based on viewings of the recent spate of mummy movies that man-eating scarabs (based no doubt on the behavior of *dermestid* beetles) were moderately useful to the gods of fate in dispatching bad people, and I have noted that they generally emerge when greed is displayed. Carry a bag of loot out of an Egyptian tomb or even think about it and poof—up springs one of these babies ready to chomp. There is no evidence from ancient times that scarabs were carnivorous or that they were particularly opposed to greed, although they seem to be useful as insurance against stinginess, which is a far more widely practiced behavior. In ancient Egyptian texts, scarabs have a strong solar significance (as in the beetle pushing the sun disk into the sky), and the divine beetle Khepri is conceptually related to the notion of "becoming," not destroying.

The beetle Khepri is really a big help to dead people in the Egyptian mind-set, which sort of implies that people after death were seen by them as tantamount to some kind of fertile dung. As abhorrent as this thought seems at first, it is not unlike one's older relatives asking to be put into a "green garbage bag" after an inspection of the paltry remnants of their 401Ks.

The Book of the Dead prescribes scarab
beetle amulets carved of dark green stone as
protection against decomposition of the human
heart. Since the Egyptians also believed that the
deep conscience and intellect resided in the heart
(not in the head), adding a scarab amulet became
a way of keeping human emotion under control
so that the resurrecting dead person was enabled
to remain relatively stress-free during the
grueling interrogation that the Egyptians felt they

would go through, one involving a tribunal of 42 assessors. In other words, the scarab helped you avoid making a fool of yourself in court.

Edgar Allan Poe's classic story *Some Words with a Mummy* (1845) implied that only Egyptians of the highest status were entitled to wear the so-called Scarabaeus, although in reality, the Egyptian magical system called for all mummies to be outfitted in this way for purposes of regeneration. Poe also played around with the idea that you could apply electricity to a mummy in order to resuscitate it. Poe's fictional mummy Allamistakeo is awakened in this way, has an extended conversation with some silly 1845 intellectuals interested primarily in making Brave-New-World banter, and after listening for a few minutes, I think quite rightly decides to sink back into unconsciousness. Allamistakeo was no fool; he just wanted some sleep. The scientists in the story are more than a little cowed by the ancient Egyptian's mental prowess compared with their own, so after he fades out, a second jolt of electricity is not applied.

I sometimes wonder whether Poe had been right about the power of electricity to wake the ancient dead, and I even suspect that mummy experts secretly tried to do this at least once or twice back in Poe's era. At the same time, I think that the world seems a little too focused on bringing mummies back to life. We'd probably just embarrass ourselves in the process and be in real trouble if we actually succeeded. What would we say to them? Wouldn't the exchange just sound like Joey Tribbiani from *Friends* talking to Shakespeare? Wouldn't we run a risk of offending somebody?

Modern person 1: "How <u>you</u> doin'?"
Mummy: "*Weneni wenenet sedjer eki*" "I was
  indeed sleeping."

Modern person 1: "Huh, er what?"

Mummy: "*Mek res enek wey*" "Behold, you awakened me."

Modern person 1: "Huh?"

Mummy: "*Djedi mek wey!*" I said: here I am!"

Modern Person 1: "Can you go slower; wait, read this, I've written my question in hieroglyphs using crayon!"

Mummy: "*Depet nebet aak sey!*" "All taste is perished."

Modern person 1: "Please have a look at this scarab, a guy named Morry gave it to me!"

Mummy: "*Mek wey er nehem `aa ek sekhty*" "Behold, I will take away thy ass, peasant."

Modern person 2: "Oh great, now he's not saying anything! Try shocking him again."

Modern person 1: "How about a storm of peaceful scarabs to show that we mean him no harm? Oh never mind, I think he's really dead. Isn't it interesting how light in this room looks different than it does in the den?"

Chapter 9

Creative Surrender

Bureaucracy, Ancient and Modern

There was a time when I thought that 23 + 42 equaled 15. I discovered this while going through a stack of old tax ledgers that were left in my mother's garage. Deftly fitted in between the ledgers, I found a stash of my math exercise sheets from second grade. Analyzing the first sheet that came into view, I felt my reactions change from moment to moment. The teacher's evaluation of my performance was indicated at the top in red ink. The pen of its frustrated writer had obviously torn into the paper and had likely dug into the surface below.

I have an unusually strong ego, but I felt a tinge of embarrassment when I realized that the "P" in the word "POOR" written here was a full 2 ½ inches high. (I keep a small tape measure handy to speed assessments of this kind; most of us with strong egos need to know for certain that the disapprobation of others does not reach a full 3 inches). My mood changed to one of pure happiness upon seeing that I had gotten two of the 32 answers on the sheet correct on the first try, and rose to the level of sheer elation upon discovering that my exhausted second grade teacher had made an error in grading one of those two answers "correct" when in fact it too was wrong. Just knowing that the poor woman had herself made a mistake and never caught it made me so much happier.

Nevertheless, this teacher had me so terrorized about getting something wrong that I often tried not to hand my work in, period. After months of tutoring, I eventually learned how to add correctly, but I knew at this point that I would never make it as a banker. However, yesterday (August 6, 2011) being the very day on which US bonds were downgraded to +AA by Standard and Poor, I was made to wonder whether the real issue confronting our society is that we choose as our bankers people who think 23 + 42 equals *115*. Where are all the teachers?

Teachers, for all their importance to our world and inestimable knowledge of their subjects, are usually reduced to the level of bureaucrats in order to do what they do. This should be kept in mind when we criticize them for their limitations as people. I doubt my second grade teacher wanted to be as mean to me on a personal level as she actually was. How silly of me to presume that I was more than a plus/minus, unsatisfactory/satisfactory on some piece of paperwork that she was required to submit monthly. In spite of her enduring villainy, she deserves our forbearance. I think her name was Mrs. Zalesky. I'm not sure she was ever a child herself, so she deserves our compassion.

Bureaucrats get a bum rap. I have been one from time to time in my career, and I have even had to be mean. I can tell you that if you have it on your list to become a bureaucrat, you had better be ready to yell at times. Yelling is often necessary to keep things from getting ridiculous or even dangerous. At least that's what bureaucrats tell themselves. If people think you're nice all the time, they'll walk all over you. Now this doesn't mean that we should fire on crowds in Tiananmen or Cairo's Tahrir Square and stuff like that. There comes a time in the lives of all bureaucrats when they need to come to terms with the fact that their game is up and they should let the natural energies of the universe just wash over them. It's called Creative Surrender. Imagine this as a new type of cereal, trademarked as the "Breakfast of Bureaucrats."

To paraphrase the poet Shelley, "On the back of the box, these words appear: Feeling half-sunk? Suffering from shattered visage? Try new *Creative Surrender*." It's a great way of conserving energy and it really beats saying things like "let them eat cake."

If eaten every day as part of a
conscientiously applied program of nutrition, just
one bowl can be an effective way of avoiding
being tried for crimes against the state while
lying on one's back on a hospital bed inside of a
cage at the age of 83 (a fate to which Hosni
Mubarak was recently subjected).

I love *creative surrender.* Not only does it
keep people out of trouble, it's also a significant
source of riboflavin. Sadly, I cannot patent it
since it's by no means something I can claim to
have discovered. I came upon an instance of this
kind of thinking in an unexpected place years
ago while I was doing research on a group of
tattered old documents written in the hasty
cursive form of hieroglyphic handwriting called
hieratic. The documents are collectively known
as the Reisner Papyri. They were documents of
dizzying complexity, quickly prepared by

professionals who were good at this kind of thing—true bureaucrats, one might say.

The Papyri are named (as papyri often are) after their discoverer who in this case was the famous American Egyptologist George Reisner (1867-1942). Reisner, a Harvard Man who wore spectacles, looked like a bureaucrat, but had a tough side. His long and prestigious career included a stint coaching the Purdue football team in its legendary second season (1889, a two-gamer). His players crushed the team fielded by Wabash College of Crawfordsville, Indiana. The other game that season was a loss, however, and possibly in an early instance of the principle of *creative surrender*, Reisner chose to let the natural energies of the universe flow in upon him and left Purdue to get some much-needed sleep. To this end, he renewed his commitment to the scintillating study of Semitic languages. Soon after, however, his natural desire for thankless conflict reemerged and he gravitated toward Egyptian archaeology.

Reisner was a man of his era. He may have modeled his appearance after that of Teddy Roosevelt (another Harvard Man who wore spectacles). Unlike Teddy, however, who eventually tired of tobacco, Reisner liked smoking a pipe.[22] This was not his most attractive habit, but it doesn't seem to have put anybody off, either. I'm not sure what brand of tobacco he used, but it couldn't have been that terrible because, although almost devoid of practical digging experience, he did well in the money-raising department too. For at least six years, he benefitted from the financial support of the mining heiress Phoebe Hearst. I want to say that Phoebe was an important person in her own

---

[22] Teddy Roosevelt quit smoking the cigars that his father had compelled him to adopt.
http://motherjones.com/mixed-media/2011/02/worst-presidents-smoking-correlation

right, a great philanthropist and not just the mother of a famous newspaperman. Reisner had a flush period, 1899-1904, funded by the paper residuals of Phoebe's immense wealth in dug-up silver, copper and gold. This gave him the time he needed to learn how to dig and record things well. Choosing out-of-the-way places to dig, he eventually found the papyri lying in a coffin in a 4,000-year-old grave.

The work of these ancient writers clearly demonstrates that Egyptians might not have been the first bureaucrats in history, but they were clearly some of the most innovative. The Reisner Papyri are believed to date to the time of King Senwosret I (1960 BC) and already we see perfected in them the specialized techniques of bureaucrats and accountants, featuring above all else, spreadsheets filled with columns and columns and columns of purportedly meaningful notation. These things look really official and answer all the deeper questions of society. How does one manage a big pyramid building project while it's being built? Answer: with columns and more columns of meaningful notation. And how does one manage the damned thing after it's built? Answer: with columns and columns of meaningful notation and oh yeah, loaves of bread. A huge amount of this meaningful notation deals with the bread needed to pay all the workers. Bread was a very big deal in Egypt. It got people to sign onto some pretty harsh duty. Have a disgusting canal that needs dredging? Start baking some bread.

My wife, a reformed bureaucrat, provided me with needed grist on an important issue. Ancient Egypt had nothing like what we see today, where benefits exist in many workplaces allowing people to be not just well-fed but over-fed and provided with ample leave time for purposes of having bariatric surgery which should usually not be needed in the first place. On the other hand, without this level of humanitarian complexity where leave is parceled into sick, vacation, and compensatory days (some but not all of which is transferrable to next year), at least four out of five benefit specialists would be looking for work and therefore not have the ability to eat so well themselves. Without the large number of benefit specialists to pay, the payroll specialists would probably dwindle in number or at the very least, need to tabulate their own leave time.

At this point, my wife returned from the supermarket complaining, justifiably, about inflation.

By far the most interesting aspect of the Reisner Papyri is the way they show that ancient Egyptian bureaucrats were already forced to deal with worker displeasure at being bureaucratically handled. In them we see a fully developed strategy of workers going AWOL. The papyri are full of calculations of how much work can be done, given that this or that number of workers are not present on a particular day to actually do anything. In other words, work increases or shrinks based upon who and how many people show up at any particular time. We have all had the experience of being in a restaurant when key staff people aren't present. It usually means that an otherwise fine dining experience is completely ruined. Food is cold or takes too long to come. We all feel ignored and probably were. This is clearly a flogging offense, but in doing a little research on how the military views someone who is AWOL, I learned that people more or less get away with it.

Although there is not a huge amount of information suggesting that ancient Egyptian bosses paid anybody particularly well in the first place, these documents establish something absolutely crucial for us: they prove that at an exceedingly early point in world history, people had the freedom not to show up for work from time to time, and more importantly, that the system couldn't do much to stop them from not showing up. Creative surrender.

In an odd twist of fate, soon after Reisner discovered the papyri, Mrs. Hearst delivered the news that she could no longer afford to support his expedition. Conventional Egyptological wisdom tells us that this occurred because of a failure of a Hearst gold mine. To me, it's interesting that Phoebe's withdrawal of major support (1904) coincided with the great period of labor unrest in American mining. The momentum at this time was decidedly against the unions; workers were constantly being shot, shot at, or deported to other states if they showed the slightest interest in organizing themselves.

My feeling is that things were so bad in places where Phoebe had mining interests that she diverted money from the bespectacled Reisner, who was finding fragments of a culture which had formerly existed in Egypt, and put her money instead into promoting culture in places where it had always had trouble existing in the first place: the American West. Phoebe funded library construction in Anaconda Montana and sponsored cultural edifices in other hellish mining zones as a way of counterbalancing what the dastardly Pinkertons were doing on behalf of stockholders. Did the workers in the Homestake gold mine (South Dakota) in 1904 have half the rights that one of Senwosret's workers did in 1960 BC? Did someone ask for some sick leave? One can't help seeing that dreadful saloon keeper Al from nearby Deadwood rising to the occasion even though his own days were numbered in 1904, using foul language that would curdle cream and an army of thugs to whip everybody into shape. Say what you want about Al, he had good bureaucratic instincts and kept excellent spreadsheets, though he gives all of us with unusually strong egos a pretty bad name.

I like much better the unknown scribe who penned the Reisner papyri. This guy really knew his business, too. It's not enough to just give the workers some bread. Let them be where they want to be once in a while. If we put enough columns and numbers down on the sheet, the boss won't even know that they're gone. Will it matter that the pyramid is finished a year late? You know, maybe he never turned in his work at all. I sometimes think that even bureaucrats have a heart, that's why the whole spreadsheet mess went into a grave in the first place.

Chapter 10
Beer and Circuses

Potent Potables and their Role in Academic Funding

A good friend of mine (a respectable professor with immense scholarly gifts) recently spent a few days in my neck of the woods with the ostensible purpose of working on a grant for a small amount of research money. Historically speaking, I have never liked working on grants or indeed on any project which poses a threat to my complete independence. Yes, of course it's nice to receive money ahead of time for work you think will make the world a better place, but just knowing that the granting agency will want a full accounting of everything later on is just too stressful. I don't want anyone thinking that I'm involved in a boondoggle, and call me immature, but I believe that a lot of grants are for boondoggly things which sound great on paper, but are of dubious merit.

As my friend and I discussed different budget categories and typed figures into an Excel spreadsheet, my brain voice began saying things like "Can't we invent a new soft drink (like a Piña colada, but preferably a little less milky) and sell it by the glass to raise this money instead?" or "Hey, can't we just work at Arby's for a few months to make the money? I used to do this when I was a kid and they really paid. Besides, we can subsist cost-free by quickly swallowing leftover roast beef sandwiches before they're deposited into the dumpster out back."

As my body's systems began rejecting the idea of asking a heartless agency for money, I felt parts of my brain drying up in a process called "neuron-crisping." It's brought on when I am under threat of being perceived as a responsible citizen or when I am asked to engage in productive activities. These things run counter to my natural inclinations. I can be productive only when I am not asked by someone else to be productive. The neuron-crisping increased when we ventured out at "break time" to have a few beers. It happened that there was a large supermarket down the hill from the hotel where my friend was staying, which had a pub built into it and a fairly extensive beer selection. It had become traditional in academic circles to "brainstorm over beers," and I knew that my friend would insist that it was time to drink up for victory and indeed illumination.

I suppose the idea that beer consumption is related to brilliance and that it leads inexorably to major funding could stem from the fact that in 1921, Danish physicist Niels Bohr successfully roped in support from the Carlsberg Foundation which was built on brewery profit. Out of sheer respect for the practice of "brainstorming over beers," I contend that research will eventually show that the ritual originated as copycat behavior based on a seldom-discussed event dating to the later phases of Prohibition, in which an anonymous drunk claiming to be a university physicist discovered a light green blob that reminded him of raw deuterium while waking up in an alley puddle behind a New York speakeasy. I would like to imagine that the conversational cycle at the first true "brainstorming over beers copycat event" began with how the light green blob had matured rapidly, applied on its very own for funding and even had a shot at admission to the periodic table. I would similarly like to think that it ended with disclosure of the fact that the committee in charge thwarted the blob, kept it off the bloody table and denied it even a partial stipend.

In any event, I knew that I was doomed to undergo additional neuron-crisping over the next few hours, even though our surroundings were more or less pleasant and really nothing was going to be expected of me beyond interesting conversation. As portions of my brain slowly emulsified, several memory neurons accidently fired off images of ancient Egyptian brewers I had known, straight off the tomb wall, so to speak. I imagined them doing a taste-test of Upper Egyptian light ale, a potent combination of river water, choice 6-row barley, exotic malts, and just a smidge of fermented honey. It was a favorite among the crews that built the sun-temple of king Ny-user-ra, but only because the overseers handed it out for free. Connoisseurs later commented that it had the mouthfeel of the mortar used in construction.

Just as I had reached the point where the editors of the *Ancient Egyptian Beer Advocate* pronounced this brew to be "of the Nile but certainly vile," I noticed that a group of loud women had parked themselves next to our table.

Awakening fully from my Egyptian beer fantasy, I quickly picked out the leader of the group, a 40-ish woman who was sun-tanned to a color resembling the beer in my glass, a hue of tawny copper made much richer in her case by the complex interweave of tattoos that covered the right side of her body. She meant no harm, but she inspired a fair degree of terror in me, in part because of the four-letter words that ushered forth from her mouth every few seconds and because she resembled Quiqueg, the frightening Maori warrior in the novel *Moby Dick*. Quiqueg had always scared me as a child, and facial tattoos still had that effect on me decades later. It took years of therapy to snap me back to my senses, and the fear of Quiqueg subsided only when I realized that he looked a lot like the old comedian Phil Silvers, but with more tattoos.

As the women at this table began drinking, they got louder still. What were they really after,

I wondered? Perhaps they were the last of a dying breed of cannibalistic Amazons last seen in the late 4th millennium BC, and only weaned off man-flesh with the invention of grain-fed domestic cattle and the limestone graphic novel. Would the leader come over to our table, I thought? Would her obvious physical superiority expose us to the whole world as merely beer brainstorming academics instead of the infinitely more fearless class of people who drink in the middle of the work day while thinking deep thoughts?

As she approached us, I thought: Would not noble Narmer himself, "Master of the White Crown," have feared this woman, and lo, would he not have hired her on the spot and added her to his ever-expanding army of mace-wielding warriors dedicated to unifying Egypt? As she opened her mouth to speak, I checked for filed teeth or deliberately accentuated canines. But she

merely smiled and asked if there was an ATM
nearby, as she needed quick cash.

We pointed toward the door, she trotted
off and we ordered another beer, as this was
essential to our on-going scholarly discussions.
Beer in fact had become a way of life for several

of my favorite Egyptologist friends, and I had learned how to hold my beer in order to be retained within their circle. It never really seemed to matter that I knew anything substantive. If I was able to accept them for themselves and provide designated driver services in the event that they needed to be dragged home, that was quite sufficient. Still, if there are any lingering doubts as to the value beer has for the scholarly community, let these be forever dismissed. Here are some noteworthy archaeological beer episodes for the reader's consideration:

Episode 1: An early mentor of mine spent regular installments of his grant monies on cases of a modern Egyptian beer which must, I am sorry to say, remain completely nameless. Quality control being questionable at the time of this expedition, some of the bottles had germinated and begun to sprout interesting mushroom-like growths that exuded an aroma not unlike burnt melon. On the night before beginning the work, I realized that I was being trained to drink beer at any cost in order to show that I was up to leading an adventurous archaeological life. Proving myself equal to the challenge, I quickly pulled at the mushroom as if it was a grenade pin, and freeing the bottle's mouth of most of the encumbering fungi, drank deep. The result of this experiment was "the grenade rule" —the discovery that the bottle should have been ejected from the hand after pulling the pin and prior to imbibing. After a stupor lasting about 17 hours, I was fit for archaeological service, which consisted largely of clearing razor-sharp grass and fly-infested cow dung from a mysterious mound.

Episode 2: A later mentor of mine declared that we could sit down over a six-pack and crank out a dissertation proposal and determine my life's work. Before I could protest effectively in favor of actual thought and consideration, he pulled out a case of that beer of dubious quality control for our rapid consumption. Upon espying a mushroom-like growth and a whiff of burnt melon, I changed my dissertation topic and left on the first train out of town.

Episode 3: My all-time favorite Egyptologist friend, a real adventurer whose generosity was legendary, took me on an all-night tour of the beer establishments in his home town. We had a grand old time, impressing barmaids with tales of Egyptological adventure, but this led to an introduction to a professional wine aficionado and part-time lingerie salesperson. She was quite cute, but, upon inspection I saw that she was tattooed in the manner of Quiqueg. I ran for the door.

All this confirms my belief that beer consumption is an absolute prerequisite for success in any academic endeavor, grant-writing included. Please know that I am fully committed to helping write any grants you may have out there that need writing, and I will do so free of charge. My money's on you guys. By the way, does anybody want to buy a bottle of this sports drink I've invented—it's less milky than a *piña colada* and comes with a free roast beef sandwich.

A Brief Commercial Interlude

Chapter 11
The New Science of Inevitaballistics
Art and Time Travel

I recently arrived at an office where I am a frequent guest, and a friend (much younger than myself, but prematurely very, very gray) announced that someone had just proven that time travel was impossible. My first reaction was to think: "Thank God! It's already crowded enough around here without some time traveler coming in whenever he pleases." But then I thought: "This is really serious. If somebody important or relatively smart declares the time travel dream to be dead, it probably will get that way." After all, who has the time to re-do the math or even understand the other guy's formulaic constructs: all those deltas, sigmas and italicized lower case letters that seem lost in a scrabble, but when assembled unchallenged may alter the latter day. Has the day arrived when we must admit defeat and erect the Henry V-like marker that says "time travel died at such a place"?

Consider these crucial sentences popularized by the Pre-Socratic philosophers: "Things tend to change." "All things change." "Change is inevitable." "It was inevitable, I suppose, let's have a drink." "Mommy, I stepped in the water again, but it looks different—waa." These are important observations to be sure, but has anyone thought about what all this means and what can be done about it, I mean beyond just having a drink? We need to figure out how things become inevitable in the first place. And more especially, we need to discover how the inevitable can be rapidly and seamlessly avoided. This is not simply a matter of twisting historical facts and pretending that things happened differently than they did, as fun and profitable as that can be. The task before us calls for a "circumvention philosophy" which will make it possible to avoid the unavoidable.

There should be a study (a new science, really) taught at universities, distinct from history, that deals specifically with change as a circumventable reality. I would call this *inevitaballistics*, the science of "penetrating the inevitable." At its core, this philosophy would hold that there is a tipping point before which a particular change might <u>not</u> occur. It would be the duty of all those trained in the methods of this new science to identify tipping points. Imagine the crest of a wave just before its rollover occurs.

How does this differ from history? Tart it up if you will, History is really about what happened in the past and why those events took place—the science of what happened. In contrast, *inevitaballistics* is about avoidance, pure and simple. The *inevitaballister* (I promise never to use that word again) would dissect events to discover the critical moments of reversibility. In the words of the immortal Eliot (J.P. not T.S.), "Do not ask who is it, just refuse to make the visit." It is practically needless to say (but I will) that the "aha" experience of *inevitaballistics* is represented by a key human thought expression: "I can still get out of this." In theory, we should be able to avoid lots of really bad stuff this way. If we return to the wave analogy for a second, the moment of reversibility would be located at or near the wave's zenith. If you see a zenith coming, run the other way, or at least begin stopping. Any step beyond the zenith will lead to the rollover effect and will eventually lead to its opposite, the nadir.

This is the extent of my understanding of celestial mechanics, although I will mention that it has recognizable origins in the calendars of ancient Egyptians and links in with their magical ideas regarding predicting good and bad days. One may say that idea reached its zenith in the mind of the deterministic philosopher Laplace sometime around 1824, the point at which he announced that although big things were nice, he was becoming interested in other things called molecules. Although I cannot prove this, I think Laplace's interest in molecules was itself a tipping point. He never wrote on the subject, eventually sickened and died in 1827, a personal nadir for him without a doubt. I even think it possible that a "3-year rule" exists in human events. It goes like this: after a zenith is reached, it takes about 3 years for the associated nadir to occur. This is really an argument against retirement. Take the following example: Napoleon reached his apogee of power and stomach size in 1812; he reached his nadir in 1815.

The 3-year rule, was, I believe, especially in force for anything reaching its zenith in 1824.

For those doubting the existence of this rule, consider these intriguing and persuasive examples: In the field of music, Beethoven wrote the 9th symphony in 1824, eventually sickened and was dead by 1827. In the field of early Egyptology, Henry Salt, not overly famous but nonetheless an important British diplomat at Alexandria, reached his zenith as an antiquities collector in 1824, also eventually sickened and was dead by 1827. In the field of poetry, Lord Byron diverged from his normal track of rapacious dissolution lyrically delivered, to boost for the Greeks, sickened ahead of schedule and was already dead in 1824. No one can contest that he was in even worse shape by 1827. None of these guys avoided much and would not have made good *inevitaballisters.* OOPS!

I like the idea of time travel. It allows me to believe that I can leave the dreary present and enjoy myself in other eras far more charming than our own. Don't get me wrong, the present is great, especially from a sanitation perspective—all that clean recycled water, flush toilets, and all manner of quality air fresheners about. As an Egyptologist, I can't help mentioning the importance of air fresheners in the ancient world. What were frankincense and myrrh really for back then if it wasn't about making life more pleasant for those that had no room at the inn? Then there's the fact that in ancient times, when the tomb of King Tut was new real estate and freshly sealed, somebody broke into it to steal, not so much the gold, but the incense with which the boy king had been buried.

Anyway, back to my litany of present day advantages. Can anyone beat the eating that goes on these days? The health conscious gourmet has a veritable cornucopia of luscious foods to choose from. Without a doubt, the present age offers a tremendous array of tasty and inexpensive delights laden with just the right amount of high-fructose corn syrup to dazzle the palate. What days these are! What days!

The big problem with the present can be summed up in three words: It isn't charming. OK, four words. When did the world cease to be charming? Was the death of charming avoidable? Some would say the end came with the start of World War I —the guns of August. I can see why they say that; gray uniforms caked in trench mud did not have the charm of good ol' Prussian blue. And then there's the direct testimony of people living back then. Take the following conversation (one of many we can imagine spoken in October 1914). "Hey Otto, who took mein pants stripe und helmet schpike? I vas counting on zem to make ze afternoon assault more charming." Yup, 1914 certainly was the end of something. But I must insist that the cutoff date for charming was 90 years earlier. On the basis of my earlier examples, the world of the charming probably began to sicken about 1818 and crested in 1824, the year that Louis Daguerre began playing around with his *camera obscura*. It was only a matter of time before the processes of true photography were turned into a juggernaut crushing the essence of the charming under its potent wheels.

Now, after a huge amount of analysis in which a thimbleful of data was amassed on this topic, I have come to the conclusion that charming has something to do with being somewhat but not entirely wrong about whatever it is that you're concerned with. I once saw this terrific old print (I love old prints) with images of birds and centipedes, palm trees and things which purported to be scientific. In my estimation, it must have been drawn by someone with virtually no eye for detail at all. It was filled with so much pictorial whimsy and apparent *make-believe* that it was more or less worthless to the scientist, but had all the earmarks of a great work, not artistically mind you, but by virtue of what the artist was incapable of drawing because he/she could not believe what he/she was looking at or asked to depict while creating a huge number of encyclopedic volumes for some Scrooge-like insane publisher. Plainly under a time crunch, the artist must have made things up, and in the process of producing pure error, he created something charming.

This genius is Andrea Bernieri, who illustrated the monumental work *Il Costume Antico e Moderno*[23] by Guilio Ferrario (1767-1847). This publication was put together between 1818 and 1826. Its popularity continued for decades, I think in large part because of Bernieri's beguiling art work. The 3rd volume on things

---

[23] Guilio Ferrario, *Il Costume Antico e Moderno o Storia del Governo, della Milizia, della Religione, delle Arti, Scienze ed Usanze di tutti popoli antichi e moderni.* Asia Volume VII, Terzo dell Asie, 1818.

Asian is particularly charming. On the one hand, Bernieri must be regarded today as the master of wonkiness. On the other hand, he succeeded in doing what no other artist has managed to do: he tastefully set back the rules of depicting reality by at least 2,000 years. It is difficult to distinguish his work from that of a medieval Irish monk or a mosaic artist working in Byzantine Ravenna. Clearly, it is the wonky quality of Bernieri's drawings that should immortalize him and set him at the forefront of echelons of great graphic illustrators since the beginning of time.

To me, Bernieri is the next best thing to a time traveler and is therefore a creature to be studied in depth. The unrealistic anatomy of his human and animal figures, the nearly complete absence of convincing perspective (both geometric and atmospheric) is something to behold.

While we moderns, debased by the
ubiquity of photography, may be moved to
declare 3 days subsidized target practice on
Bernieri's work, we must restrain our vile
emotions and instead pause to consider all of the
rules he has wisely avoided. There is not a single
image published by this man which disturbs the

viewer. Can the same thing be claimed of photography?

Photography has its tremendous merits. It gives us a semblance of accuracy and truth. It makes great evidence in a court of law or in the field of science. Nowadays, it is instantaneously transferrable, postable and sharable. But is it the most effective salve for the human spirit? I would answer: as a rule, no (photos of favorite pets and children may be a rare exception). Give me a Bernieri any day. It may just be that in his peaceful wonkiness, his undying respect for the charming, Bernieri reveals himself as a mysterious Prometheus who has stolen the knowledge of the inevitable from the gods themselves. This is one time traveler who can come into our present whenever he pleases.

Chapter 12

Milky Eyes

Combating Ancient Evil with Buttercream

Rarely a day goes by when I do not stop whatever I am doing to find a quiet space in which to kneel and thank the gods that I was born with a good head of hair and a smaller-than-average stomach that makes it pretty near impossible for me to overeat. I usually complete these rituals with the line: "And oh yeah—thanks O supreme, impersonal, universal power for not giving me a milky eye."

This is not intended to be a criticism of people with eye problems. I myself descend from weak-sighted people with Coke bottle eyeglasses. This is really about the common human fear of not being liked by many people, not for any egregious deficiencies of our own, but because of an unavoidable physical characteristic disturbing to others at a primal level, like a milky eye. No, I am not talking about the disgusting trend one sees a lot on YouTube these days of people inhaling glasses of milk and squirting the milk out the corners of their eyes. I am talking about real superstitions which polarize society, now forgotten horror—the dreaded Evil Eye of ancient times. It's like that "pale blue eye with a film over it" which the old man had in Poe's famous story *The Tell-Tale Heart.* Had not this disgusting eye driven the narrator mad? Had not a simple case of keratitis, easily curable with topical antibiotics, gotten the old man killed?

In order to better understand this phenomenon, I consulted Alexis, my illustrator, asking her whether she had ever encountered someone with an evil eye. "Oh yeah, somebody I knew at college had a 'stink eye.' " Never having heard this term before, I asked her for greater detail. She discoursed as follows: "Whenever this girl got upset, the eye just got stinky." I determined through additional questioning that the term "stinky" when applied to an eye meant that it began to tremble uncontrollably based on the owner's state of mind.

Still feeling myself to be in the dark, however, I asked Alexis for even more detail; I can be rather thick at times and I like to ask precise questions to tease out unrecognized truths. "Did you coin this term 'stink eye' or did you get taught it somewhere?" To this Alexis replied: "All I remember is that this girl just had a stink eye." Attempting again to get the heart of the matter, I asked: "So did you make this up?" "No, she (meaning the weird girl at college with a trembly eye) told me ahead of time that she had a stink eye, and I learned over time to recognize it as it was going stinky and to avoid her altogether when it did."

"Stink eye" it turns out is a perfectly acceptable and widely used term among surfers, who are apparently now viewed as experts in recognizing the nasty and disapproving looks of those around them. It may have its origins in the Hawaiian language, but there's hardly a culture out there without some equivalent. As far as American culture is concerned, though, I think we have lost our way with respect to the entire evil eye concept. In other words, to most of us, evil eyes are simple stink eyes, the proverbial hairy eyeballs which we send to those we despise.

Consider the following sentence, transcribed into *adolescentese*: "It's like he's really weird, so I gave him a stink eye, and he like left." This concept of the evil eye is way too innocuous. Any way you cut it, we have to face the fact that evil eyes are not something we can turn on and off at will; you've just got 'em or you don't, and if you're so afflicted, everyone else tries to avoid you, rightly so.

When I think on America's misunderstanding of evil eyes, I sometimes think of Jason, you know, creepy "Goalie Mask Jason" who went around senselessly killing everybody in all those movies. Sometimes you could see his eyes even through the mask, but most of the time we couldn't quite make out whether he was giving us the evil eye or not. Only too late we realized that he had been. Horrible Jason. It's amazing how many people started naming their children "Jason" after that string of movies came out. If we were a more superstitious people and had any seriousness about evil eyes at all, we would have banned the name altogether.

The ancient Egyptians to be sure had strongly developed ideas about evil, but generally speaking, eyes to them were good or at least reasonably neutral. An eye might be considered "dim" or "weak" (i3rr), but not evil. The most famous of the Egyptian eye symbols was the *wedjat*, the whole or "sound" eye of the god Horus. This eye was overwhelmingly good; some even think that the Founding Fathers, many of whom were Free Masons, were impressed with the idea of an all-seeing, all-knowing eye, and insisted that it be incorporated into the seal of the United States and affixed it as a symbol on US currency. At any rate, the myth goes that the eye of Horus magically repaired itself after being grievously injured by the decadent Seth, lord of storms and chaos. Other sources tell us that Seth knocked it out of Horus' head altogether. The Eye came back soon after, fully healed. In another version called *Papyrus Chester Beatty no. 1*, Seth, who more and more comes to resemble *Goalie Mask Jason*, removes both of Horus' eyes and buries them up on a hill where they sprout as lotus bulbs. This is a pretty bizarre myth at the get-go, but it gets even worse. Eyeless Horus is deemed fixable by the goddess Hathor who proceeds to milk a gazelle. This gazelle milk is poured into Horus' eye sockets and lo and behold, both his eyes are healed.

Now, I don't mind the fact that his eyes healed properly, but the fact that random gazelle milk worked like magic suggests that even way back in the time of Ramesses V, which is when *Papyrus Chester Beatty no. 1* was supposedly written, the vast dairy syndicates were already hard at work spreading the message that curds and whey could do us no harm. There was even an Egyptian milk goddess and powerful corporate spokesperson named Iat. I assume that she was generally friendly, but judging from the appearance of the texts, she may have been a kind of vulture.

I recently heard a recording of Julia Child, mistress of French cuisine, commenting that in America, cream had gone from something chic to something that people have become scared of. I would never attempt to besmirch Julia Child. She was her own person, defending cream on its own merits, not because the syndicates told her to. She believed in the power of cream to improve most any dish. To me, she is a goddess of the hearth who, like the Egyptian cow goddess Hathor, felt deep down that all our woes could be solved with precious milk.

Julia Child died at almost 92 in 2004. If she had been living 3,200 years ago, she would be counseling all of us to whip up some yummy treat like *French cream filling* or ricotta to stuff into Horus' injured cannolis. I can see the headline now: "Archaeologist discovers papyrus in ancient kitchen." It reads as follows: "Recipe: whip up cream from one heavy gazelle, fold in the white of one egg (preferably vulture) and add vanilla extract until inebriated. Serves one eyeless Horus, or two Horus' with only one eye. A favorite with the whole family —amazingly fluffy and decadent."

"Decadent" is a major baking word. Seth really lost out when the bakers seized hold of his one special attribute and made it their own. We're all allowed to be decadent when it comes to dessert. In fact, I'll go out on limb and declare that it's okay to be decadent as long as the things we're decadent about are also fluffy, especially if it's your birthday. Even vegans, the evil eye outcasts unfairly shunned by the rest of modern Western society, feel this way. Take the following example paraphrased from a vegan website, kept nearly the same as the original to increase the comic value: *A mouthwatering non-hydrogenated delight: Have some fluffy vegan buttercream frosting on a decadent gluten-free cupcake.* I think I'll avoid the gluten-free version of "decadence" on my next birthday.

Back to fluffy. If it's fluffy, it probably also involves incredibly sweet and fattening foods or lots of coconut oil. The word "fluffy" sounds good with most other words except possibly when it precedes "residue." I may be in the minority here, but I find that particular word combination to be somewhat unappetizing because it catapults us from a world of dietary sensations into one filled with images of oil-eating microbes doing strange things with their mucus near the zones of a major oil spill. Fortunately, investigation of the ancient Egyptian language by all manner of expert linguists has failed to discover an equivalent of the words "fluffy residue." We are not quite so lucky regarding "mucus" (nšwt) and we mustn't forget those related favorites, saliva (iš) and "spittle," the latter always a popular word in ancient civilizations where the need to publicly castigate others by means of bodily efflux was always coming into play.

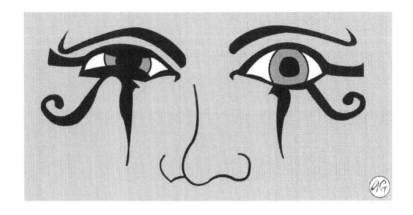

To ancient Egyptians, the spittle factor was so important that they had two distinct words for it (šw and psg). I respect the Egyptians greatly, but I don't make distinctions where my own spittle is concerned. In their world, however, I suppose that the enormous stresses of daily living brought functionally-specialized spittles to the forefront. One of these types might have been reserved for flinging at ancient strabismus sufferers mistakenly believed to be casting the evil eye. The other would be for all those daring to question the prevailing dietary orthodoxy: "Load up on buttercream until you can't see straight. Horus would approve."

Chapter 13

The Riviera Maya

Vacations, the Fantasy and the Reality

Today the headline read: "Explore Mysterious Ruins and Stay at a Luxurious Resort." A picture of the famous Mayan pyramid temple of El Castillo at Chichen Itza beckoned. "Poor Chichen Itza," I thought. It's difficult to avoid the conclusion that the world has been turned into a massive theme park. Now, I know this isn't really fair to say and I certainly don't want to be unfair to Chichen Itza of all places. I grew up enthralled by it despite an inborn distrust of the surrounding rainforests and swamps, and I remember getting extra credit in 7th grade math class by drawing El Castillo relatively well, despite the bleed of my Magic Markers, on a poster articulating the fine points of the Mayan numeral system. They had the number Zero, written like a coffee bean. My child life was filled with happy dreaming about this place, this temple city hidden among the palms, a vestige, some would say, of mighty Atlantis, or at least its Western Branch. This old idea fueled the pioneering research of John Lloyd Stephens and artist Frederick Catherwood who in 1839 hacked their way into temple-filled Mayan cities, long abandoned to the Yucatan jungle.[24]

The hawker's bill went on: "The ancient and the modern: You can have both in the Riviera Maya. Save up to 46% on your dream vacation today." It was hard to argue with the costs. It was one of those trips just slightly more expensive than staying at home. The hotel had been thrown in for free. In fact, it was a lot less than the trip I had just booked to go to less-than-sunny Tacoma, Washington for a week of back-

---

[24] Published as Stephens, *Incidents of Travel in Central America, Chiapas and Yucatan* (1841); followed by *Incidents of Travel in Yucatan* (1843); and as Catherwood, *Views of Ancient Monuments in Central America, Chiapas and Yucatan* (1844).

breaking work, fraught with horror. I figured that my airfare alone for the Tacoma trip paid for the roundtrip flight and three nights in the Riviera Maya.

But if I weakened and went to the Riviera, would I really be exploring anything? Looking up El Castillo on the internet, I determined that the exploration factor would be reduced severely, perhaps to a trickle. The Wikipedia article, for instance, included the important fact that visitors were no longer being permitted to climb the stairs up to the throne room at the top of the pyramid and had to be content walking around the base.[25] The visiting public could not go into any Mayan chambers of any kind, and this rule had been in place since 2006. I had missed my great opportunity, years of Egyptology having interfered with my travel to the Maya heartland. El Castillo would go unclimbed unless I could

---

[25] http://en.wikipedia.org/wiki/El_Castillo,_Chichen_Itza; visited August 29, 2011.

wrangle a quick marriage to someone like Jennifer Lopez, who was granted "unprecedented access" to El Castillo on April 2, 2011.[26]

Ms. Lopez's visit seems to have been part of the Federal Ministry of Tourism's larger strategy of getting the message out to the World that great archaeological sites exist in Mexico and that they should be visited. I imagine that the folks at the Ministry want these visits to occur sooner rather than later and this might explain the incredibly affordable rates. Ms. Lopez, wearing a beautiful diaphanous gown, was carefully placed on the central step structure of El Castillo about seven steps up from ground level. She looked ravishing and her very high heels matched the color of the stones exactly. Her film crew made it up to the eleventh step, possibly to videotape her back. They looked decidedly crumpled, the huge "N"s on the side of

---

their New Balance running shoes matched nothing.

The video is clever and beauteous advertising for something that does not fully exist today, but one day soon might: an archaeological theme park where all is pleasurable and convenient. The editing conveys the impression that El Castillo lies about 100 yards from an ocean with beautiful beaches and that muscular bodies will emerge from the waters on cue to provide a mixture of love and intriguing light grooming services on those exploring the temple. It is true that the Mayan site of Tulum lies on the shores of the beautiful Caribbean in Mexico's Quintana Roo State, but the pyramid of El Castillo is a different matter altogether. Chichen Itza is, in fact, 45-50 miles from the nearest coast and this is not the coast most visited, nor is this calculated "shortest distance" one traversable without machete and three barrels of defoliant.

What would my trip actually be like, I wonder? Would it be what I hoped: a romantic adventure with light grooming of an intriguing sort, punctuated by flights of fancy amidst the smoky ruins of once-mighty kingdoms of staggering dimension? Or would it be a touristic nightmare among mangrove swamps, the likes of which only duck-hunters and tarpon fishermen could enjoy? Mangrove vacations are admittedly of great value, and their value, in my limited opinion, is established on the basis of the ease with which they lend themselves to being poked fun at. Nevertheless, recreation in swamps where human beings are not needed or wanted is undertaken again and again under the banner of the adventure vacation. This being said, I consider it likely that many venture to the Yucatan without the slightest intention of braving the jungle or the swamps. The average conversation while viewing pages on Expedia or Orbitz, peppered with photo thumbnails of hotels named "Playa this" or "Hacienda that" would go something like this:

"Typed in *Yucatan, Flight and Hotels.* Nothing. Got something under *Playa del Carmen,* wherever that is. Let's see. Hmm. Here's a good package, the place has a large pool, and we can even take day trips to ancient sites like Tulum or Chichen Itza. Wait, there's more. It says: *4 ½ stars.* Good. Wow, look at this—real marble floors and a gracious concierge to make traveling an absolute dream."

Unlucky with vacations, I began imagining my arrival at the hotel *Playa Whatever.* Brief contact with the concierge (a splendid fellow) revealed, however, that even absolute dreams have their limits. The average temperature in September was 90 degrees, relative humidity 81 percent. I was quickly informed reprovingly that light grooming behavior, be it intriguing or otherwise, was not included in the standard package. I had missed the morning meal, but in the spirit of the absolute dream, the concierge asked me "Would you care for a poached baby mangrove crab? There are several left at the buffet." As I awoke in a cold sweat, I realized that this was way too exotic, way too swampy for me.

My dream vacation in the Yucatan, fated to go unadvertised and without a music video, would feature the following luxuries: a string of unfettered, heartfelt 'Good Mornings' from a happy staff, followed by a decent breakfast featuring granola in place of mangrove swamp fauna, and a supply of reasonably absorbent cocktail napkins to stem the tide of sweat dripping from my fetid brow. With these simple pleasures, I can handle the *rain forest*, but I aver that such things should never be taken for granted. Save them, yes, but know that in saving all those trees, we multiply only our own discomforts if we choose to live among them. This truth the Maya already knew I'm sure, and chose to leave Atlantis for the beach. The concierge from my dream popped back into my mind's eye temporarily. I glimpsed him eating, in the way one would an oyster on the half shell, the poached crab which I had avoided earlier.

I have no doubt that for the Lucky (that is to say, for people who know how to arrange terrific vacations for themselves and actually enjoy them without dyspepsia), this trip to the Riviera Maya would be a peak experience. They would depart from it refreshed with bonus points and frequent flier miles all meticulously recorded and remembered by the great Rewards bureau in the sky.

I speak for the unlucky. I speak for Edward H. Thompson (1856-1933), the archaeologist who, more than any other American, made a home in the Yucatan and helped to uncover Chichen Itza and then had his plantation there nationalized by the Mexican government, only to die in Plainfield New Jersey. OK, $75.00 US wasn't really a fair price for a Mayan metropolis.[27] I speak for the archaeologists of bygone times who weren't smart enough to stay away from jungle temples. I speak for all those who, in search of immortal fame or some intellectual El Dorado, perished for want of a little quinine, only to have the world of their explorations taken over by real estate magnates. More importantly, I speak for those plagued by dyspepsia which hits them always at the wrong time and usually as a result of eating poached mangrove crabs. And last of all, I speak for all who come to explore Chichen Itza and find nothing other than El Castillo as eye candy, J. Lo

---

[27]http://www.planeta.com/ecotravel/mexico/yucatan/tales/04 11explorer.html, Jeanine Kitchel, Explorers of the Yucatán, retrieved August 30, 2011.

having long departed. Depressing. The Maya didn't invent Zero for nothing.

Chapter 14
West of Java - A Tropical Low
Climate Cataclysm and the American Workplace

This essay is being written on August 27, 2011, the anniversary of the eruption of the island of Krakatoa. I, eschewing anything that is cliché-ed, will not stoop to declare that Krakatoa was actually west of Java, but said to be "east of Java" in order to help market a cinematic melodrama about the 1883 cataclysm filmed in 1969. Nor will I become so pathetic as to name members of its cast, which incidentally included Maximillian Schell and my favorite actress, Diane Baker. Ms. Baker had, just seven years earlier, survived Hollywood's original Battle of Thermopylae (*The 300 Spartans*), avoiding the worst aspects of its screenplay and emerged healthy despite being barefoot while traversing the rocky terrain of Thessaly and Phocis.

This storyline meander went on cinematically for hundreds of miles, allowing Ms. Baker and her young Spartan boyfriend to make their rendezvous with destiny at the battle of Hot Gates only by dint of intense podiatric suffering. I would have soaked my feet in bubbling springs upon arrival if I had been them; the Thermopylae area was full of upwelling vents, although Greece's main volcano (Dafni at Santorini) was farther off and had blown its stack 1,000 years before the events covered by the movie. This famous blowout (and its attendant tsunami), known as the Thera Eruption, destroyed the best aspects of Minoan culture and was so traumatic in its consequences that many see in the collapse of sleek Cretan palaces the true inspiration for legends regarding the submergence of Atlantis.

By strange coincidence, the Krakatoa film (*Krakatoa, East of Java*) starred another actor associated with bare feet. This was none other than Rossano Brazzi who, in one of his earlier movies, had to play a guy with a terrible war injury (not to his feet) which made for a depressing wedding night for a raven-haired contessa who, as a teenager, was frequently seen in Gypsy road camps dancing around without footwear. This beauty danced away the hours fancy-free apparently as oblivious to the gravelly terrain as she was to the fact that she was the only good-looking woman in a camp of thirty adult males.

But this is pure digression. Krakatoa is indeed west of Java (but it is also arguably east of Java if one is willing to travel very, very far). Today is also the day that a hurricane named Irene is expected to make landfall along the eastern United States (also considered to be west of Java, but could be east of Java if one is willing to pay for gas). Everything seems to be on the verge of falling apart right now, but this is really nothing new. In fact, as I write these words, I am sitting in the very chair on which I sat during the August 23rd 2011 East Coast Earthquake which caused my oaken office floor to become like hot putty at exactly 13:51 EJST (east of Java standard time). If this is truly the end of our world, I can possibly get my dibs in and be the first to compose a timeless account of the debacle. Pliny the Younger managed to do this during a badly-timed vacation visit with his uncle during the eruption of Vesuvius in AD 79 and it did wonders for his book sales. What my career needs now is a truly terrible disaster. Day 1: I see a smoky-looking cloud on the horizon; Day 2: the smoky cloud is getting bigger and I have to look straight up to see it; Day 3: either the cloud is really big or it's 9:30 at night; Day 3.25: I just got hit in the left earlobe by a menacing pumice particle—that kind of thing.

I may come off as a pessimist if I say this, but things are indeed bad for all of us most of the time. Never mind the fact that we all managed to survive the eight other hurricanes that were floating around the Atlantic this year— this one's gonna be the grand-daddy of them all. Never mind about those bloody grand-daddies. The events of Hurricane Sandy proved that the grand-mommies of them all could be much, much worse.

In an earlier discussion, I led the reader though a maze of thought regarding "circumvention philosophy" which I termed *inevitaballistics*, the new science of deconstructing inevitability, which is perhaps better described as *the new science of avoiding the unavoidable.* Although an initial cogent *inevitaballistic* analysis revealed that the entire philosophy should just be discarded, I couldn't avoid thinking that it needed to be looked at again on the off chance that it might just be worth pursuing. How would I behave if faced by a major cataclysm, something like Vesuvius, the Thera Eruption, or Krakatoa? In other words, if I know something out there is going to erupt, would I have the good sense to deal with it constructively? Failing this, would I at least know how to get out of its way?

Eve entered the room at this stage and, in an oddly serious frame of mind, commented that the word "Krakatoa" was underutilized. I queried her on this, asking what the word "Krakatoa" should be used for. "It should be used to describe a category of human experience," she answered, adding: "I just don't think it's used as much as it should be." I could tell that she felt strongly about this, but ignoring her gravity, I tried to be funny in order to improve her mood. "You mean it hasn't been turned into a hackneyed phrase yet?" Sensing that I should tread carefully because she had just woken up, I managed to sputter anemically: "Don't get me wrong, I like hackneyed phrases—they're great!" This pathetic attempt at facetious backpedaling merely accelerated my collapse. She declared: "I'm going off to the post office to mail something."

Never one to avoid further difficulty, I threw out a quick challenge: "Wait, we're not done talking about Krakatoa yet!" Only slightly perturbed, Eve turned to me and said: "OK, if you must know, I would classify "Krakatoa" with words like 'crucifixion'—also underused. People say 'crucify' a lot, but they don't say 'crucifixion' very often. I recall that a brain-fried attorney I knew once used 'witch-hunt' and 'crucifixion' to pretty good advantage in fiercely and irrationally resisting our efforts to help her to maintain an even keel. That attorney was one impressive chick, completely crackers, but impressive."

Crucifixion? Witch-hunt? Where was my wife going with all this? Again deciding to "step in it," I said: "Maybe you just like nouns." But then I thought about it. Krakatoa was to her a metaphor for the problems at her former place of employment. All those problems seemed to erupt at once and propelled her into "escape mode" (reminiscent of Diane Baker hopping around near Thermopylae), avoiding the workplace equivalents of hot ash and pumice at every turn. She decided to leave her job in the spring of 2010 in order to preserve her own mental health once it became clear that the main brimstone activation chamber there would never grow quiescent; her boss, for years a contented sort, had become a volcano of the simmering variety which never blows sky high, but instead becomes unhappy, belches to itself, and figures out how to release ominous gases without letting anyone know the true source. Shades of Pompeii.

There is an important principle at work in the evolution of human volcanoes. It goes by the convenient acronym TITAC: "too important to actually communicate." What this means is that we human beings learn at an early age not to discuss anything that is important until the last possible moment. By then, of course, it's usually too late to affect any meaningful change.

At this point, I couldn't help but remember a boyhood trip to Italy and what a tour guide told me about the people of Pompeii as I looked at the famous plaster cast of that dog gnawing at its leash. All those Pompeiians, those who stayed behind that is, stubbornly held out in the belief that the pyroclastic flow would reverse itself and that the ash would magically stop falling. Just then, the gases got them.

Somehow, this is manifestly not just a Pompeiian thing; it's a human thing—to hedge our bets and hang out until the last possible second. This works on the assumptions that: (1) we can outrun a nature that is uniformly slow-moving and predictable, and (2) we can escape the harmful effects of that which is usually bubbling around aimlessly, venting occasional gas. Based on my examination of the Krakatoa, Vesuvius and Thera examples, the following strategies come to mind:

First: The spewings of mountainous cones are generally bad and one should sell the family homestead, even at a substantial loss, when confronted by the remotest possibility of cataclysmic eruption.

Second: When it comes to human volcanoes, try communicating as soon as a problem seems to break the surface—don't let noxious gases build up.

Three: Avoid all tsunamis by never taking vacations.

Four: Leave all mementos to be discovered by later archaeologists. None of your younger relatives want the stuff that we think is so important, not least of all, Uncle Al's early voice recordings.

Fifth and most important: Never leave the dog behind! Most beloved pets I know are worth more than the stupid house.

Chapter 15
The Horizon of Thoth
Clairvoyance and New Age Archaeology

It's a real shame that contact with spiritual forces has fallen into disrepute. This situation has gone so far that trips to mystics are out, and we have our other-worldly wisdom handed to us whether we want it or not, usually after we have eaten too much, through the medium of the obligatory Chinese fortune cookie. I have been quasi-addicted to low-grade fortune cookies for years, and in a disturbing trend, have seen a steady dropping off of their original prognosticative value. The decline might have something to do with the crowding of new forms of information on these tiny strips of paper. These elements distract us from true awareness of the universe.

First, we have the Chinese vocabulary loaded onto the back side of the paper. This at the get-go is just too demoralizing to be borne. Can any one of us English speakers have a decent future once we find ourselves incapable of remembering even simple terms in Mandarin such as "hello" or "one"? In Asian terms, we are all completely talentless and unemployable, unfit to manufacture the sneakers on our very own feet. My particular downfall was the Chinese word for "potato," a vegetable that I detest to begin with, and even more so since it became an apt description of what remained of my brainstem after trying to remember the word while digesting four spareribs thrown in too hurriedly on top of a pint of won ton soup.

Another modern pollutant threatening occult inspiration are those suggested lottery numbers intended to replace the mystical formulae arising out of our own life experience. My own lucky number is 56 and I discovered this in the fifth grade under circumstances that cannot be re-told. The only question is whether any lucky number actually works more than once. I don't want my lucky number to be proven ineffective, so I never play it.

Finally, the fortunes themselves are becoming too "everyday" and more like advice rather than real fortunes. Come on, admit it, a Chinese fortune cookie nowadays is capable of telling us to "Eat right" or "Watch your cholesterol." Just last night, my fortune was reduced to a measly two words: "Don't Panic!" I had no thought of doing so up to that time and began to wonder whether the chef at "Mr. Chan's Dragon Buffet" had inserted a warning to accompany my order, *pork lo mein* produced some three days before.

Where do these fortunes come from, anyway? One theory has it that a small man in a room behind the lobster tank in Chan Lung's Chinese Kitchen off 9th Street in Philadelphia has been employed for years writing these things. According to Alexis, he was once paid as much as 25 cents a day for this highly skilled work, but was recently subjected to a cut in salary to a mere 10 cents, hence the decline in fortune quality. Another theory has it that the information on the small paper strips comes from Atlantis. I have no direct evidence of this, but I continue to look. I think that the word "potato" may be a clue; I must point out that this vegetable was originally native to the New World only and was completely unknown to the Chinese. Is there a single potato in traditional Chinese cooking? I ask you, is there?!

Things we are familiar with seem to betray us when they turn out to come from someplace unexpected or weird. I recently found out (don't ask how) that the Anglo-Saxon Chronicle maintains that the ancient Britons originated in Armenia. Their nasty neighbors, the Picts (an ancient tribe, well known to Prince Valiant which I would have thought dwelt in Scotland) apparently sailed over from the region called "Scythia," which on antique maps fell somewhere in the old Soviet Union. While I want to favor the idea that a potato-eating Atlantean was responsible for my fortune (probably his way of wanting me to finally accept potatoes as both nutritious and delicious), I am sensitive to the reader's natural skepticism on this issue. Besides, my respect for Thor Heyerdahl inspires me to suppose that a potato could have floated from South America in Inca times, up the Yangtze to Nanjing and been cultivated secretly for their blossoms on the imperial estates of the Ming. Everything was perfect probably, until one was cooked and eaten, which may explain why the capital was moved to Beijing.

Let me just say that I long for the days when fortune-telling was firmly in the hands of the Egyptians. From remotest antiquity, Egypt has deserved its hefty reputation as a center of learning, and it is clear that the pharaoh ruled a nation of libraries filled to the brim with divine words recorded on papyrus. Besides, they sure knew what to do when it came to creating cryptic knowledge which is almost impossible for modern individuals to understand. I have been fixated on this simple fact for years and love to read Egyptian lore, particularly when it is late at night and the world is quiet. It is then that ancient Egypt speaks out in mysterious sentences and in my view, comes to life for the Egyptologist. It is then and only then that scholars long silent come forward out of books and tell their stories. This experience furnishes an alluring main dish of occult morsels to me, without too many spiritual potatoes.

I particularly love reading about the West's "discovery" of Egypt and thrive on quaint

accounts of early travelers there: Paul Lucas
(1699-1703), Reverend Richard Pococke (1737-
42), the artist Luigi Mayer (1792) and soon
thereafter, Bonaparte himself. Bonaparte did the
most of all of these, establishing the Institut
d'Egypte and promoting study of the Nile valley
which, in the year of his landing (1798), was
more a field for fables than realities. Say what
you will about the militaristic Napoleon, he
deserves acclaim for having the foresight to have
bundled scientists into his expedition to Egypt.
The work of these men brought the 23 volumes
of the *Description de l'Egypte* into being. It is an
amazing contribution to world culture and a real
turning point in the history of scientific
publication.

It came as something of a shock to me to
learn in mid-December (Dec. 17th, 2011) that the
building chosen to house the literary product of
Napoleon's expedition and so many other

important documents went up in flames in downtown Cairo. The building housed a lot of maps, and my feeling is that whoever torched the place had an ulterior motive. Egypt practically invented "the library," but we can't escape the fact that it also explored library fires pretty thoroughly, too; no matter how much Caesar's spin doctors try to convince me that the scroll-fed flames in Alexandria were caused by the lads of the fleet whilst toasting marshmallows, I think it pretty likely that the destruction of a huge number of land documents might have been the goal. There's no better way to avoid debate than to burn old deeds.

In order to get my mind off the pile of ashes that once called itself the Institut d'Égypte, I turned to the important subject of Egyptian magic and esoteric knowledge. In the days before the fire in Cairo, I had discovered in a fragment of a real Egyptian document the expression (please say with a steady, awe-inspiring intonation) "Horizon of Thoth." These words on first sight look to be imaginary—totally Hollywood and not worth the fake papyrus on which they were penned—but in point of fact they were really there. Next to them were several other words written in hieroglyphic symbols, unfortunately of uncertain meaning.

I never expected this and yet it occurred (please say with steady, awe-inspiring intonation). Indeed, I would expect to find such language in a mummy movie (but only those of the less intelligible variety) with characters drenched in latex and with screenplays crowded with mythological phrases concocted at the end of the 19th century by séance organizers, wishful thinkers, and manufacturers of tarot cards. But there it was, the expression: "Horizon of Thoth."

What could this be? A gateway to ancient wisdom, perhaps? A repository of hidden lore—the source of all magic? Was the text a fragment of a rare *Hermetic* text—on papyrus?

Hermetic Who? The background goes something like this: because of his magical powers, the divine scribe Thoth (who the Egyptians connected with the ibis) was a favorite of fortune tellers and clairvoyants. This insanely long tradition began in ancient times when the search for new sources of magical power drove the Greeks and later the Romans to dig deeply into other peoples' cultures for strange stuff—and who could beat the Egyptian idea that the most powerful magician afoot had the head of the bird with the world's longest beak? Although the ibis is by no means a swift bird, the notion that Thoth delivered divine telegrams got him associated with the Greek god Hermes (messenger of the gods). Hermes could deliver messages, but he was no lover of the mailroom and eventually ran away. Thoth, however, developed a taste for organization and liked to hang about in libraries.

A popular prophet named Edgar Cayce (1877-1945) helped popularize the Thoth-Atlantis link. Cayce's great contribution to New Age sensibilities was the connection he made between Thoth and Atlantis. In Cayce's theories, Thoth was identified as a kind of engineer who managed to escape from the cataclysm which doomed Atlantis before recorded history, went to Egypt and got involved in pyramid construction on a massive scale.

Now, I happen to think that Atlantis is one of the sketchiest places on earth. The reason seems to be that years ago in antediluvian times, the actor Patrick Duffy, needing to make a living, accepted the role of the sunken city's sole survivor who somehow rose from the deep by swimming like a tadpole in the year 1977. To judge from the 13 episodes of his brave but sadly doomed series (*Man from Atlantis*), the Lost Continent's only cultural influence on the present world was bad hair. In a cataclysmic vision which should have been seen by Edgar Cayce, the entire planet would be submerged by waves, not of salt-water, but of badly styled human hair. And how could it be that the "sleeping prophet" never saw what followed in the wake of Atlantis' disappearance? Namely, that just a few short years later, a new race of men developed for whom the code of masculinity required pompadours and tresses blown-dry to such incredible proportions that only contrastive polka-dot shirts with over-sized collars and rust-brown corduroy three-piece suits could look good beside them. Such a development, involving millions of living beings, blow-driers, and enough lethal aerosols to destroy a thousand ozone layers should surely have filled the dreams and visions of an army of prophets. But did it? Absolutely not.

Anyway, back to Thoth. Thoth wrote lots of books and these became a great repository of knowledge, which, according to Cayce, lay in a great Hall of Records located below the Sphinx at Giza. This wonderful, romantic idea is still widely believed in, and indirectly inspired the research of Egyptologists such as Mark Lehner, the current expert on ancient goings on upon the Giza plateau. Part and parcel of New Age beliefs is the idea (possibly derived from Plato's *Critias*) that Thoth's Hall is a creation of great antiquity, perhaps on the order of 10,000 years before present, more than twice the time assigned to it in "Conventional Egyptology." The New Age crowd maintains that the Sphinx predates the surrounding Pyramids substantially, but would have inspired their construction by teams of Egyptians empowered by engineering methods extra-terrestrially derived.

Some hold on so jealously to this notion that they are potentially dangerous to themselves and to others. I once curated a small Egyptian exhibit which had a fragment of red granite from king Menkaure's pyramid in one of its display cases. One day, a visitor arrived who had a question for the curator. She happened to be a well-regarded pianist of some renown. In fact, I had once attended a concert at which she had played and I had enjoyed it thoroughly. What a cool lady! So I agreed to give her a quick tour.

She lingered by the fragment and asked my opinion regarding how and by whom the pyramids were built. I foolishly presented the conventional idea that Egyptian rulers of the Old Kingdom commissioned these marvels, and cited the existence of Khufu's cartouches in red chalk on blocks above the king's burial chamber in support. This engendered such outrage that I quickly dove for cover from the pianist, who, in movie fashion, had transformed herself into a spitting cobra. How could an ant like myself possibly believe that human beings had built such things without the guidance of a superior species?

Fortunately, the concert was timed so as to preclude further application of New Age venom. As a scientist, I felt hurt and slightly misunderstood, but at least I was safe. First of all,

I am not against the "mystic's view." It's the basis of romanticism and I really like the idea that people can see things that I cannot. I believe in such things as meaningful coincidence, powers of prognostication and different forms of wisdom. It's nice to think that someone out there is in direct contact with a rich store of knowledge that can remake the future, and indeed, that the key to a more perfect world is out there just waiting to be discovered in one of my favorite places.

Had I stumbled upon the sole evidence of Cayce's vision? We might never know for sure. I can only speculate on its impact on all those minds waiting for a sign from on high, like that particular New Age composer. Still, as much as I feel that the evidence might create problems should it fall into the wrong hands, I cannot bring myself to destroy it. There has been way too much fire in the world of late. I only hope that the future sends me a sign, and that the Horizon of Thoth, wherever it is, is not in Idaho.

Chapter 16
Just Too Much
The Juggernaut of Modern Advertising

My wife and I recently went to the public library to pick up a DVD, and I was dismayed to find the penny book rack filled with old National Geographic magazines. The yellow margins of these well-known "improving monthlies" glowed in the late afternoon sun. I was moved to examine one or two, but was dissuaded by the small but steadily growing feeding frenzy around them. This incipient swarm was swelled by those who, I conjectured, plainly had had the money to have subscribed to the Society, but had chosen all these years not to, probably on the theory that there would always be periodic disgorgements of National Geographics flooding into penny book racks across the free world. In this case, they had wagered correctly that they would always be granted access to random issues completely free of charge or nearly so. The only price exacted from them would be the penny per issue to defray the cost of library operations or possible embarrassment at a future cocktail party. The latter expense would be incurred if and only if the acquirer would be moved to describe aloud something just learned from one of these issues, which everyone else at the party had known for decades.

These were not the really old National Geographics one loves to look at, the ones with non-pictorial white covers with the tables of contents printed on them and old advertisements on the back, usually for Coca-Cola. These were more recent National Geographics, the ones that have much better photography and a distressing paucity of written text. By the way, when it comes to National Geographic advertising, the Coca-Cola era was roughly 1935 through 1945. This was the era of "refreshment," the drink's tagline being *the pause that refreshes.*" Take these three examples: "Desire (thirst and a longing for cooling refreshment) is the reason why ice-cold Coca-Cola is ready to be served at more than a million places." (June 1935).[28] "Wherever your schedule may be, ice-cold Coca-Cola adds the flavor of refreshment to a welcome pause." (October 1941). And finally: "Wherever a U.S. battleship may be, the American way of life goes along . . . [29] in sports, humor, customs and refreshment." (February 1944).

---

[28] I was astounded to discover in an advertisement of this antiquity the following information: "Coca-Cola is a pure drink of wholesome, natural products, with no artificial flavor or coloring, complying with pure food laws all over the world." This interest in product quality seems somehow inconsistent with the advertising artwork featuring an exhausted prospector mopping his brow in the company of a burrow or pack mule thirstily eyeing an unassuming cactus. Certainly the cactus would exemplify a wholesome natural product with no artificial flavor or coloring, but I wouldn't recommend drinking from one.

[29] These three dots, present in the original, are of uncertain meaning. To me, they are extremely portentous, nay, sinister.

But why do these piles exist? Are we to suppose that the subscribers are themselves completely disgusted by the publication? My explanation for this state of affairs is not that the magazine has declined in quality, although I would say to the editors that making photographs huge no longer impresses the savvy minds of 21st century westerners, most of whom have digital cameras with immense megapixel capability and even SLR cameras as good as any in the NG equipment closets. Nor do I think that the writing itself has become facile, although the captions in the magazine border on the idiotic, particularly when juxtaposed with overly huge photographs. In my view, the problem has nothing to do with the mechanics of the magazine, but has everything to do with the degenerating state of the mechanics of the planet. The age of discovery has clearly ended and has given way to the age of discovering that we shouldn't have discovered things to begin with. Remember what I said earlier about the poor dodo!

As far as the declining mechanics of the planet are concerned, I claim no special expertise, but can draw certain conclusions based on looking out my own front window. I live in a small and not too prosperous town that has had the good fortune to have become the hub of the logistics industry in the northeast. It is the kind of place that is simultaneously the "middle of nowhere" and the "middle of everywhere." I have the distinction of living on the wrong side of town and am therefore a witness to an unceasing and absurd parade of goods headed onto our nation's highways. Most vehicles navigating my street are oversized and arrive in flotilla, a veritable "catalog of ships" laden, not with Achaean heroes, but with all the future detritus of our present world: cool Ranch-flavored

Doritos in bulk, energy drinks in the thousands and a favorite of mine: stackable pre-fab sections of Lego-like hotels wrapped in energy-efficient Tyvek.

Most of the drivers are good people, but, sadly, entirely incapable of avoiding an eight-inch pothole located 40 feet south of my house. I call it the Pit of Hell. Mesmerized by the monotony of the road, they direct their tires into this pothole, and by doing so, create vibrations equal to an attack of the *Luftwaffe*. They remain incognizant, of course, despite the visible failure of the masonry bonds of the 1880's house adjacent, now shaken to its foundations. Despite this, the imminent loss of that poor structure is more than compensated for by the knowledge that my fellow citizens will be able to indulge their every consumerist fancy and keep our economy humming. The objects bought are undeniably important, for it is through them that the lives of people here go on peacefully and happily amidst the crushing wheels of inexorable fate. (Foley artist: insert "crushing wheel sound" comprised of the following sonic elements: over-inflated mammoth-sized truck tire outfitted with iron chains rolling at 15 mph over a full case of aluminum beer cans, preferably Budweiser).

At the same time, there are benefits to living in such a place to people interested in understanding historical processes (and in writing the archaeology of our times), for this place is truly a microcosm of modern America. The goings-on in this town almost defy description. My wife and I quip frequently that we live in a medieval village not unlike those that dotted the hills of Tuscany in the early 14th century. In our town, it is possible to take a walk down shady lanes, comforted by the presence of beautifully-kept stone buildings, only to have the bottom fall out from under you. Conversation would start out something like this: "Look, honey, at that decorative corbel. What a nice detail. They don't make them like that anymore. Such craftsmanship!" followed by: "Look at the dappled sunlight on that lovely brick wall. This is an eternal moment!" Five minutes later, we can turn a corner and come face to face with that woman who we all know from her timeless image, fingers brought up to her mouth, wondering how to feed her children in the first years of the Dust Bowl. This is why there's no better place to live than where we do. An average day's juxtapositions here are worth a hundred truckloads of National Geographic anywhere else. Now, if you'll excuse me, it's time for a Coke.

Chapter 17

Three Pages Too Far

eBay Shopping and the Voyage beyond the Absurd

A good friend of mine named Randy laughs every time he sees or hears the word "grotto." He has an unshakeable belief in its inherent silliness and told me so during a drive southward toward Manassas, Virginia to help his daughter relocate to that area. I went along to help him lift and move her things. As it happened, the highway passed a religious site known for the sanctity of its grotto. Randy insisted that I take a picture of the sign announcing it so that he could laugh at it later on, and I went along as best I could, although at 75 mph, my photographic efforts came out as a blur.

As an archaeologist, I have a healthy respect for the word "grotto," since it is linked to what we now call the "grotesque" after the

Renaissance discovery of some strange frescoes and sculptures in the-then-subterranean world of Roman ruins. I can imagine myself venturing into some grotto in 1450 with the great humanist architect Alberti (1404 –1472) to see newly-revealed works of pagan antiquity for the first time, taking it all in, trying to assimilate every bizarre fragment and to gain from the experience. It made no difference to Alberti whether he was looking at debauched snapshots of the Saturnalia—he was going to benefit from it, and by God sir, he did.

Is it possible to have this experience today? Can we have a moment of glorious wonder like those enjoyed by Alberti and discover in the handiwork of alien minds buried in a grotto below some non-descript pile, splendors both illuminating and liberating to our imaginations?

As an experiment, I decided to shop for a piece of art on eBay; my feeling is that items of beauty are still out there, ripe for discovery, and I am an optimistic explorer when it comes to real art. The terms of my search were simple: I typed in the word "portrait," hoping to chance upon a charming mezzotint in gentle tones—blended sepias that calm the soul in trying times like these and worth every penny. I recently came to appreciate mezzotints while chancing upon a landscape with satyrs dancing around a lake, an 18th century rendering by Earlom deftly following the 17th century master, Claude Lorrain.

What I retrieved in my search for a decent buy was disconcerting. My chosen search term dredged up 2,485 pages of self-proclaimed portraits, a staggering 137,096 separate entries. After about eleven pages of "looking," I grew nauseous in the way that only prolonged surfing on eBay can induce. My eyes no longer worked in concert. I had become a chameleon with independently rotating conical turrets instead of eyes.

My search had made me ashamed to be a human being. I couldn't believe how many bad (really un-redeemably ugly) portraits have been created since the year 1600. A lot of them were anonymous female nudes (many of perfectly gorgeous Chinese women), but even these I found unattractive owing to the hideous intermix of monkey and horse portraits I encountered in between. These mocked the viewer at every turn, but further looking had elevated their position, as if the never-ending cascade of human portraits of doubtful dependability made one long for the loyal equine. I began to wonder at the motives of the artists and about the character of their models.

Along the way to these visual treats, I came across two recently done paintings of Czar Nicholas II in imperial uniforms, one in green, one in white (perfect for one's dining room); a great Dane (or perhaps a boxer-mastiff) wearing an imperial uniform in red; a portrait of the comedian Jon Stewart called by its artist "an abstract," perhaps to hide the fact that it looked nothing like him, and a well-rendered but implausible image of Oliver Cromwell's mother, who I seriously doubt would have allowed herself to be painted at all, even if the artist promised to supply her with multiple Warts. This, by the way, contrasted nicely with a seated image of Joseph Stalin smiling at the viewer with the innocence of Jepeto. Worst of all was the portrait of the actor Mark Harmon as he appeared while playing a character known as Leroy Jethro Gibb, some kind of investigator for naval intelligence. Need I say more?

Yes, I need to say more. I reject the notion that we must automatically accept that *beauty is in the eye of the beholder.* We may not be able, nor should we want, to stop people from buying bad art, but bad art is definitely out there sucking up the world's resources. eBay is living proof of the existence of art-blindness. My recent experience among the "portraits" category is a case in point. As if it is not punishing enough to see assassinated Czars and Soviet dictators side by side as though at a Halloween party, we must also just barely survive seeing things purveyed as "Art" that defy all logic. My favorite painting in this class is a nude of a mustachioed Polish senior citizen seated in some kind of sauna with a brass fire helmet at his feet. After digesting this horror, I also had to face the sad fact that someone out there was bidding 29 dollars for it with 2 days and 16 hours to go. Oh yeah, I forgot to mention: while forswearing any object of quality at even half this price, this particular shopper was ready to plop down 20 additional dollars for the shipping from distant Warsaw.

I was into the grotto. My search through the endless pages of portraits had gone well beyond the Absurd into a new region of thought and experience which has never been named, but which I will attempt to do now because it deserves its own label, if for no other reason than to warn the future to retreat from such things when they loom on the horizon. The Absurd is defined as an argument or thing having no rational relationship to human life. It is reserved for things so thoroughly incongruous that no one can possibly understand them. We know the Absurd when we see it and, in a certain way, we must admit that it has a poetical aspect, that is to say, it retains a kind of beauty; even absurdity can, I think, sometimes be cute. Alberti himself would have understood this, for had he not said: "There is no art which has not had its beginnings in things full of errors"?[30]

---

[30] http://quote.robertgenn.com/auth_search.php?authid=539

But what about the nether regions beyond the Absurd? It stands to reason that we have gone beyond beauty itself, even beauty of the comical sort. This area of darkness I call the *Saturn-grotto*.

My term is based upon the mythological idea that the titan Saturn, who at one time was pretty hot stuff and had initiated a Golden Age, had over-stayed his welcome so pathetically that anyone could see that he was completely past his prime and rapidly depreciating in value. At the same time, his only remaining faculty was a healthy appetite, usually taken out on his more talented younger relatives. He eventually ate most of his own children, who were only recovered through creative use of mythological enemas.

For obvious reasons, few artists wished to depict *The Rescue of Saturn's Children.* However,

retrieved 16 November 2011.

several did undertake the eating part, among them, Peter Paul Rubens. And Saturn's destructive chomping was brilliantly captured in a late drawing by Francesco de Goya. This should have been titled: *"Caught in the act—what a mess."* The image of the Polish guy in the sauna came quickly to mind, followed by nagging questions. Whatever happened to the poor fireman? Had he been devoured? Could such ugliness be repaired by painting in an ice cream cone or some other fountain treat?

As we grow older, it is important to mark well the legend of Saturn, lest we repeat the drama of his life. And here, my new term *Saturn-grotto* can be of greatest help. Usage is as follows: "The old man had to face the fact that he had voyaged beyond the Absurd and was now in the *Saturn-grotto* of his life." For those who may want to use the word adjectivally, the form can be grasped from the sentence: "After three days of non-shaving, his beard had become *Saturn-grotesque*." My pocket definition of the term *Saturn-grotesque* is: "an adjective describing a state of mind in which the beauties emerging accidentally from conditions of Absurdity are forcibly re-ordered to the detriment of visual beauty."

This is the experience of shopping on eBay. After eleven pages of searching, we can no longer judge what if anything is beautiful. Ironically, we still had that faculty at page eight, but we went three pages too far, devouring all images in our path until even we must admit we're a mess. We're like Saturn sitting in a grotto eating too much Ben and Jerry's, and there's nothing silly about that.

Chapter 18
The Fractured Knight
Vampire Legends, Past and Present

With the announcement of the death of Korean dictator Kim Jong Il on December 19, 2011, I was reminded of one of the most potent literary creations of our times: the vampire. It is now common knowledge stamped upon refrigerator magnets that these woeful creatures are fated to roam the night and, in the words of the immortal Doctor Van Helsing, "fidd an zee blud af de liffing." Speaking about feeding on the blood of the living, any aspiring author has a 50-50 chance of striking pay dirt just mentioning the word "vampire" in a book or theatrical treatment. The chances improve considerably if the author is also willing to spell the word "vampire" with a "y" as the second vowel so that the reader can, in pronouncing it, make himself sound cultured and therefore more brilliant. Try it--it really, really works! Repeat after me: "Vompier"—now swig, dramatically, an entire glass of port while standing in front of a roaring fireplace.

At this point, we know that Kim Jong Il's successor is named Kim Jong Un. Hopefully, the last element of this name is drawn from an English prefix and is indicative of future divergence from the father's pattern of behavior. What do we know of this young man? Answer: practically nothing other than that he was raised away from his father and in a place with a reputation for being more civilized than the country he is destined to rule. Uh-oh—a possible weirdo. Turn on the fireplace at once. I need to swig some port to get through this one!

Any reader managing to survive this far into my collection of stories already knows that I am fascinated by tales about dark regions inhabited by lost souls. Lost souls are really nothing without the "lore expert," a character which authors depend on to tell the reader how the lost soul became lost. They add pathos to a story which basically comes down to a case of oversized mosquito attack. I can take or leave the basic vampire. I am much more fascinated with lore experts overall. Many of these are given Dutch names, are deemed to be learned in lecanomancy (whatever that is) and are masters of medicine and medieval science. They themselves are often cursed, though perhaps not as badly as vampires are. Somehow as a result of evil forces, our lore experts with IQ's hovering between 185 and 192 are unable to master spoken English. They are fated to roam the night, replacing the "th" sound with the sound of the letter "z".

In recent years, vampire sagas have captivated many of us, especially if we are girls aged 14-25. The question is why? And can this be stopped? I discussed the issue on a freezing cold morning with my wife, who is an expert in all things Byronic and has done as much reading in the field of folklore as anyone I know. I think that Byron would have turned vampire-novelist if not a full-fledged vampire if he had stayed in Switzerland, but he seems to have bored of the whole thing and let Dr. Polidori develop the vampire stuff instead. In fact, Dr. Polidori may be the archetype of the "lore expert," but that's another story.

My wife and I spoke about the popularity of the vampire genre and began developing a concept we call "the allure of the fractured knight." It goes something like this: unadulterated good is really, really boring in a romantic sense. To make a convincing male love interest, you need to inject some charisma into a man, and this charisma is a by-product of some unstated mystery. As we all know, mysteries generally involve something sort of negative. In the case of the so-called "fractured knight," we start with someone who is superlative (indeed, almost heroic) and screw him up by introducing a fatal flaw into his character—an Oedipal family history usually works best—but sometimes in a pinch, the so-called flaws can be simple mutations. We mustn't underestimate the romantic value of weird genes. Speaking as a possessor of several, one's tendency to sprout fangs, claws and masses of embarrassing body hair during emotional crises is never fully a handicap in dating. So says the *"Lore Expert's Handbook,"* an excellent read.

Now, we all know about Bram Stoker, London-based theatrical agent for the actor Henry Irving and the modern teller of the Dracula legend. In 1897, filling the role of lore expert, Stoker resurrected his vampire out of the dust of early 19th century renditions of folktales telling of a demented Wallachian prince of the 15th century. The basic elements are well known: Dracula rises to power against all odds and tries to make good as an anti-Turkish crusader particularly skilled in impaling things. Pretty soon, though, he mucks up his own life, supposedly dies around 1476 and then spends the next 400 years biting necks and basically mucking up *other* people's lives.

The actual history goes something like this: little Dracula (Vlad III of Wallachia, 1431-76) was at a tender age separated from his princely father, who became a lackey of the Turks. Bundled off to Ottoman lands with his brother, Dracula was held under a form of house arrest to ensure his father's compliance with Turkish policies. Sadly for the custodians of the imposing fortress where he was imprisoned (yes, there is an imposing fortress involved, otherwise who would care?), he develops a set of rather nasty personal habits and a penchant for impaling things. These habits did not improve greatly once Dracula returned to Wallachia to sit as its prince.

Dracula's behavior needn't distract us too much at this point. Let us just say that unfortunately for the Turks, who were on a winning streak and headed northward into Wallachia, it meant a great deal. It meant that the expected cakewalk they had enjoyed elsewhere in southeastern Europe was soon severely off step. Captives became little more than kebabs on the table of the unstable Count, who extended little quarter and harassed any Turks coming within a league of the Borgo Pass, a perfectly ghastly location in its own right. Pretty soon, the Turkish dreams of easy conquest turned to dreams of staying home and indulging in kitchen and bathroom improvement exercises in those recently-acquired shorefront properties along the Golden Horn. Much better to voluntarily drain one's wallet at the *Bosporus Lowe's* than to get drained in the dreaded Carpathians by the merciless Dracula.

Now, my own exposure to things in Dracula's neck of the woods is rather limited. However, I have a pretty good sense of his world gained through personal experience. Many years ago "Before the Wall Fell," I had the opportunity to visit mountainous Slovakia with a college friend whose father had been born there, and I spent a couple of days in the neighborhood of a town called Késmárk, his father's home town. It was a throwback kind of place at the foot of tall mountains and had all the elements needed for a good vampire yarn. An ancient Hungarian bureaucrat trapped in the town when the borders changed served as our guide. We were shown the town church (a cold place, completely empty) and then visited the cemetery with its whitewashed mausolea. People identified as gypsies had apparently taken over the family seat, and beyond them, looming in the cool distance at the end of the main street, stood an imposing fortress, a wicked place with towers seemingly fit for breeding a whole race of impalers.

As forbidding as the place was, a little research showed my judgment to be superficial. No vampires dwelt within. The fortress had been the seat of Count Imre Thököly (1657-1705), a Hungarian nobleman of anti-Hapsburg persuasion who went so far as to join the Ottoman cause in the late 1670's. In fact, Thököly lived the inverse of Dracula's life. Left on his own by dying parents, he developed allegiance to the Turks; he fought <u>with 'em</u> rather than <u>agin 'em</u>.

His timing wasn't great, however, for after two hundred years of triumph in Europe, the Turks were at the end of their tether, tarried too long around Vienna and got themselves disastrously beaten below its walls. It was a defeat so ridiculous that even they had to admit they were pathetic. This was a good thing because nobody emerged with vampiristic goals after the battle of Vienna, and this was a very big deal: no neck biting, no coffins filled with dirt and no unnecessary trips to or from Romania. What savings!

Even when things went badly (unjustly Thököly took the blame for Vienna and became a Turkish prisoner), he managed to recover their trust and lived out the rest of his life as a member of the Ottoman court. He was never seen impaling anybody and became a frequent customer at the *Bosporus Lowe's.*

Today in this age of Smart Phones, things are vastly different. Even when one considers the distinct possibility that an app exists to allow us to impale angry birds, vampires are not without feeling. Under special circumstances, the younger breed of vampires, typified by the now-famous

"Edward" (who, by the way, is a perfect blend of Byron and Polidori, though maybe a bit pastier than either) is widely viewed as capable of having romantic feelings for others and might even be counted on to save lives! In a recent Edward movie, *Twilight New Moon*, the viewer learns that modern vampires of the nicer sort live more or less hum-drum decent lives in real families and dwell in architecturally attractive homes reminiscent of the one designed by the dad in the Brady Bunch, perfect for a sleepover.

As nice as this sounds, and as potentially friendly as they may sometimes be, things might be difficult for these refurbished vampires around dinner time, or should a life-endangering paper cut occur whilst unwrapping a birthday gift. I am told that this is serious, serious stuff. The "mortal beloved" Bella just narrowly escapes becoming the main course at her own birthday party! I had no idea that wrapping paper could do this to a person. Horror. I have it on good authority that a line was cut out of the screenplay to the classic: One of the girl vampires says: "I <u>told</u> you never to use that serrated wrapping paper at mortal birthdays!"

Chapter 19

"Get the Bag, Stupid!"

No Subtitle Necessary

I felt compelled to write this essay for philosophical reasons after strolling through my town with my lovely wife. The sun was shining brightly. The birds chirped in the style of early spring. A distant dog leisurely dozed upon the steps leading up to the door of a quaint brick house. After some moments, we reached the quaint brick house, and as the kindly dog yawned and gently retreated into its doorway, a man and woman pulled up in a car to one side of us. I noticed a roundish object on the back seat and next to it, a large brown paper bag. As the somewhat grungy, unshaven male of the pair emerged from the car, our presence startled him. In spite of this, perhaps inspired by the weather, he managed to say "Good Morning." We were impressed by the fulsomeness of his kindly gesture. Just as I began to think that all was right with the world and started to smile with renewed faith in humanity, his female companion suddenly popped out of her side of the car and yelled at him: "Get the bag, stupid!"

How cruel, I thought—how hurtful. Surely not "stupid." This poor guy just stood there and took it, as if he was used to being told where to go and what to do. I just hope that there was something *mega importanté* or perishable in that bag to help justify her remark. Sadly, between you and me, I think it was probably just some mass-market, frozen falafel.

When I returned home, I checked out stories on the internet implying that there is growing stupidity within our species. These reports warrant some discussion, I think, largely because if a plea of "no contest" is entered, we prove the stories absolutely true. The fact is that most of us remain reasonably intelligent, but are involved in some other more important activity which draws our attention away long enough to cause us to forget that growing stupidity may be a problem worth addressing, even if only for a few moments. (Foley artist: please insert sound effect of a jaw slackening on the face of someone deeply involved in texting about a beer he is not really enjoying, while a huge fiery meteor enters our atmosphere).

I'm not saying that I'm smart or anything; in fact, it's widely known that I usually have trouble telling left from right. Nevertheless, I think that a scholarly examination of the issues shows that current social trends could result in a dangerous expansion of the global stupidity quotient or GSQ. While ignoring a fiery meteor or two myself, I have been compiling a list of trends which, if not carefully managed, could expand stupidity world-wide. Near the top of the list, just below the regular buying of lottery tickets, is the phenomenon of the Black Friday shopping spree—a favorite across North America. While it is true that the day is properly color-coded to show the impact upon the nervous system, the money-saving possibilities are just too great to ignore when it comes to electronic equipment. We are willing to "pay the piper" the equivalent of several hundred Xboxes for a brain scan needed when we are seventy-six years old to determine the cause of the beta amyloid plaques invading our reduced brain space.

Farther down the list is the hallowed internet, that ready source of so much useful information. This boon to human knowledge (and I mean that sincerely) is, I report with dismay, a double-edged sword when it comes to its effects on the architecture of our brians (sorry I meant to say "brains").

Let me take you on a journey through my personal experience. In November 2012, I was tasked with creating a series of historical maps for a museum in the Midwest. Research was going fine in most respects until I realized that most of the prepared maps available on the internet relating to the subject I was doing (namely, trying to discover the boundaries of the Elamite tribal confederacy in southwestern Iran around 2250 BC) were inadequate. Most were really nothing more than a whisper-down-the-lane of some earlier map which itself had been hastily prepared and contained serious errors. After two days work, and at the point of exhaustion, I concluded that in this day and age, the locations of several supposedly important places were mere approximations. One of these places was ancient Susa, an important Elamite stronghold, later held by the Persians, *et cetera*.

Now believe me, I am fully aware that few of you out there give a pin about Elamites or Susa (modern name Shush)—and some of you may be questioning whether I have the right to exist in light of my interest in such subjects. It is certainly a sign of intact intellect to consider keeping the Elamites off your list of casual conversation topics. And mention of Susa is sure to conjure up less-than-desirable images of high school band uniforms with cheesy headgear and epaulettes, which will quickly reduce your audience five-fold, as even persons who like you take the opportunity to refresh their cocktails, or help the hostess with the dishes. In fact, my unscientific estimates show that the total readership interested in Elamite foreign policy is quite possibly no more than 28 people world-wide. Half of this "community" is angry at the other half and the remainder, wisely avoiding the petty disputes embroiling the others, speak only Swedish.

In spite of all this, I hope that you will indulge me for a few more minutes and allow a brief discussion of my research problem. It also relates to the rising GSQ. Let's begin with a simple limerick to define the basic issues at stake:

There once was a city called Susa. Its treasures are megapaloosa. While it has two large mounds and magnificent grounds, its locus is hard to perusa.

Some of you may have heard of Susa because people lived there for a long time, and eventually the place got incorporated into Bible stories and stuff like that. The tomb of the prophet Daniel is supposedly located there, which elevates its relevance, but there's a counterbalancing blow to relevance in the story about how somebody moved Daniel's body somewhere else, sometime before the year 735.

The 28 people who care about Susa probably know generally where it's located—and I will tell you that, within a tolerance of about 50 miles, its ruins can be found in southwestern Iran in the province of Khuzistan. I'm convinced that people have punted when it comes to understanding where Susa is located because of a confusing multiplicity of waterways located nearby. It seems not to make too much sense. Susa lies somewhere due east of the Karkheh River and west of another river called the Dez; it's also east of another river called the Saimarrah. The Karkheh River is also called the Ulai, which seems to be a modern form of the classical name *Eulaeus,* but it also seems that there was another name for the Eulaeus in some classical sources which is completely different: the *Cutaeus.* It's possible that no one has cared about the name *Cutaeus* since 1841.

For a dry area, the plain of Susa has an awful lot of rivers. My brain, affected probably by dreams of saving big bucks on Black Friday (now

Thursday and Friday), began doubting that the
Saimarrah really existed, but I stumbled upon a
1933 photo (on the internet) which showed it
flowing to the left of an impressive
archaeological site. Another day went by before I
had finished assembling all that I had discovered
and went to the map data provided by Google
Imagery (©2012). What a great tool.

Ah!—It makes you feel like you are really
there—perhaps hovering 50 miles above the
place—and there's no better way to introduce
yourself to an unknown place than to look down
upon it from the sky.

Once the street data show up, you can
sound like a townie and give directions to
somebody else. For example: "Just take Taleghani
Street north and park next to the foot of the
"Shush Castle" falafel stand—best in town. Watch
it, though, if you miss the turn off, you have to go

left around a mean curve and in two blocks you take a nosedive into the Saimarrah."

Needless to say, I now feel secure in the mapping of Susa. The lack of decent maps can be upsetting because it interferes with our basic notions of time and space and what's important. Pretty soon, the lack of clarity makes us stupid. I now believe that if we looked carefully at the territory inhabited by the Elamites, and examined their implacable defensive attitude toward their western neighbors in Mesopotamia, we would, despite the apparent irrelevance of such a topic, learn something major about ourselves.

Elamites in 2250 BC were confronted by powerful Akkadian rulers to the west of them. At least one of those guys liked to wear a creepy-looking horned helmet while out conquering people. Although I basically like helmets, the tension of knowing that some scary, helmeted guy is waiting out there in the valley to come marching in with his own version of what my life should be like is off-putting. I now recognize that this threat is one of the world's great constants.

Most tension, I think, arises while the brain debates with itself whether to accept the other guy's notion of what's worth doing, even when it doesn't really fit our pattern. Remember that woman who called her boyfriend "stupid"? He just stood there and took it because he feared the horned helmet sitting next to the food bag.

While it might not sound like a winning destination, I hope one day to get to Susa and to drive along Taleghani Street. I would avoid that one awful curve and eat some take-out from "Shush Castle—best in town." After lunch, I'd take a leisurely boat ride down the Saimarrah.

For the moment, however, I have my priorities straight. I'm content to do the Google map thing, travel without moving, study some Elamites and when hungry, make my own falafel.

Chapter 20

A Full-Bodied Mummy Marinade

A Mummy Wrapped in Red-Hot Tape

This story is dedicated to a little boy who sat with his grandmother in the seats behind mine during a flight to the Midwest. The little boy was super-interested in "mummies" and had a National Geographic book on the topic which his grandmother read to him cover-to-cover during the plane ride. This story is also dedicated to Adelaide and Jessica, who happened to be with me within minutes of the events recorded herein. They witnessed my pain-filled writhing and listened to my words of chagrin in recounting a discussion I had just concluded with a museum conservator about a mummy, and a kindly, but institutionally-shackled Egyptologist (a very common problem in the field, by the way, which deserves to be studied in depth).

I had an idea a number of years ago (along with Mycroft) to study mummies and burial containers originating from an ancient city called Akhmim. It so happened that I had grown up in a city which had a museum facility which I'm afraid must remain unnamed, that as fate was to have it, possessed several mummies coming from Akhmim years back. One of these mummies had been picked apart in 1973, leaving behind a skeletal object which no longer quite resembled a human being. I will spare my readers the obvious comparisons to assemblages of baby back ribs and other delicacies churned out by your local smokehouse. A few years back, the Egyptologist who later became institutionally shackled decided to do a CT scan of this particular mummy and this story made it into the media. I chanced upon the story and this led to the sad series of events which I describe for you in a later paragraph.

Now, I promise to keep this story light-hearted and uplifting. With these goals firmly in mind, I will begin again with a completely different emphasis. I will admit to the reader that I was raised in world without barbeque—except for the Chinese variety, which are generally called spareribs. I must confess that I do not know what a" baby back rib" is, and I am leery at the thought of ordering up a batch in order to find out. In a lengthy discussion of the topic with my wife, who also knows nothing about barbeque cuisine, but who like myself is interested in learning more about it, I once discussed the proper pronunciation of the term over a lunch consisting largely of tuna fish. We asked one another whether we should emphasize the word "back" or whether we should emphasize the word "baby" when expressing some imagined future order in a barbeque establishment so as not to sound dumb.

Please understand, we're sophisticated enough to understand that, regardless of which word is emphasized, we're dealing with the back ribs of some kind of baby (animal); we just have questions regarding why people insist on saying all three words as rapidly as possible, emphasizing the word "ribs". (Foley artist: please insert sound effect of someone with a "country accent" comfortable with the phrase "baby back ribs," using the words followed by some other cliché form of personal address like "y'all" or "ma'am". This expression should flow over background noises of meat sizzling and dishes being knocked together, much like the canned "diner sounds" they always play on NPR during their semi-obnoxious radio-verité-style news reports).

By the way, for anyone who's interested, the conversation between the grandmother and the little kid had, by this time, moved away from mummies into the area of the triceratops, so as I write these words, I am hearing growling sounds made by a little boy; I suppose these sounds are his versions of ceratopsians. The grandmother is now talking about the dinosaurs' chisel-shaped teeth, some of these "as sharp as steak knives." No doubt these developed to help them eat the Cretateous version of the baby-back-rib-Y'all. Boy, I'm getting hungry. By the way, the little boy has just learned that "extinct" means "no longer alive."

When I arrived at the museum the day before yesterday, I was full of youthful hope. I thought it mildly possible that after 30 years, the museum would allow Case 6 to be opened so that I could have a look at the mummy, possibly even a chance to copy the texts on his coffin, which I needed to complete a genealogy which I believed to be a reasonably important goal, one unachievable given the distance of the coffin lid from the plate glass window that separated our world from his. I had no idea what I was in for when I was warmly greeted by the Egyptologist; we sat in the museum café and chatted profitably about work on the museum's mummies that had occurred years ago.

All was fine until we were joined by the conservator. She was jazzed up about something before she sat down with the two of us, and if she wanted to be true to her actual interior state of mind, she would have torn up my well-intended but sadly doomed 3-page proposal on how the mummy could be studied. "The plate glass is very old, and if we take it out to provide access to the mummy, we will want to replace it with plexiglas." (No big deal, I thought, we should be able to get the necessary size, in modern UV-protected stock 3/8 inches thick and smooth flame-treated finished edges for around $500.00— let's rent a Uhaul and get it). The conservator continued with: "and the mummy is just too wide to fit into the CT scanner that we use. Oh and by the way, if you want to take the mummy to the scanner that you have, we will have to treat you as a borrower, and our loan fees, insurance costs, and crating charges can run into major money." (How much could this be, I thought? Possibly $10,000 or more if all was done according to strict museum procedures). I later learned from Jessica that the number in the conservator's mind was closer to $100,000-150,000 in fees (By the way, I've run the numbers and discovered that this is equivalent to 13,636 orders of baby-back-ribs, which would feed the equivalent of 13,636 normal American males, but would feed 39,000 people in any other country, 78,000 in Ethiopia).

The conservator then rose, making certain to let me know that she had two other meetings to go to, and that she had no time. She grabbed the pathetic proposal in order (I believe) to get it into the nearest waste basket without delay. Note to the reader: this is common practice among the older brand of conservators who, with very few exceptions, believe themselves to be busier than anyone else on earth. Did I say earth? I meant the Universe. What made this so irksome was that I knew better, that is, I knew that the mummy would fit into any modern scanner. I knew this mummy very well; he was unusually narrow and his coffin was among the narrowest I had ever seen. I should mention that I did have the temerity to ask the conservator if the measurements of the mummy were actually known. The disingenuous answer was: "We've eyeballed him, and he's just too wide."

I really have to thank this conservator for being born. Without her, I would not have had this amazing experience, an example of bureaucratese fricasseed to perfection and served up with a full range of tangy sauces as accompaniment. Because of this conservator, I knew that I now had all the mouth-watering fixins (yes–fixins) of a terrific first scene of a mummy movie, complete with its own brand of special morale-destroying potato salad on the side.

All of this describes for the reader the tirade that ensued in the wake of the conservator's departure. This is a version of what Adelaide and Jessica heard emanating from me over lunch in the museum café. Jessica departed and Adelaide and I went to visit Case 6 (I was still permitted to <u>look</u> at the mummy through the old plate glass, there for now 32 years). When we entered the chamber, we experienced heat on the order of high-80's Fahrenheit. Now I knew why the conservator and the institutionally-shackled Egyptologist had me meet with them in the museum café. In any house in this country, and even in some swampy state parks, the conditions in the mummy room would be adjudged uninhabitable. Adelaide, God bless her, said: "They have environmental controls in with the mummy, don't you think?" As the words "no way" crossed my lips, I noticed Adelaide beginning to melt, and as the heat reflections reached levels known only in the equatorial region of planet Mercury, I suggested that a quick exit was the better part of valor.

I still have three hopes in life. One is to see the mummy redeemed—to be properly chilled down to something resembling room temperature, and the other two are to finally understand the proper pronunciation of "baby-back-ribs" and then to eat one.